Winning with the Power of Persuasion

Mancuso's Secrets for Small Business Success

Joseph Mancuso

Enterprise · Dearborn

a division of Dearborn Publishing Group, Inc.

Publisher: Kathleen A. Welton
Associate Editor: Karen A. Christensen
Senior Project Editor: Jack L. Kiburz
Interior Design: Lucy Jenkins
Cover Design: Design Alliance, Inc.

©1993 by Joseph Mancuso

Published by Enterprise • Dearborn,
a division of Dearborn Publishing Group, Inc.

Printed in the United States of America

93 94 95 10 9 8 7 6 5 4 3 2 1

Library of Congress Cataloging-in-Publication Data

Mancuso, Joseph
    Winning with the power of persuasion : Mancuso's secrets for small business success / Joseph Mancuso.
        p. cm.
    Includes index.
    ISBN 0-79310-517-X
    1. Entrepreneurship—United States.   2. New business enterprises
—United States.   3. Small business—United States.   I. Title.
HB615.M35   1993
338'.04'0973—dc20   93-9176
                                                              CIP

Dedication

This book is dedicated to the spirit of the people who live in the great state of Texas. I've never lived there, but I'm living in Manhattan and raising two adopted children born as Texans. You'll also notice that the commentaries for this book are from two more Texans, Walter Hailey and Jim Miller.

The people in this state share some wonderful qualities. Their friendship and warmth are genuine and generous. I have never been to a single place where the rainmaker's traits and characteristics have been passed along from generation to generation until they permeate the spirit of enterprise among all Texans.

I salute all Texans. It's obvious the culture has been descended from generations of rainmakers.

It can't be described—only experienced.

Contents

Foreword

An *entrepreneur* is one who organizes, manages and assumes the risks of a business or an enterprise. All great entrepreneurs have one common thread woven throughout their successes: They all are persuasive in dealing with people. The ability to influence opinions and events is a unique talent shared by only a few. Joe Mancuso has written a remarkable book, which appeals not only to the most sophisticated entrepreneurial reader but also to the person who just wants to use persuasion as a means to achieving goals and living life to its fullest.

No one is more qualified to explore the concepts of entrepreneurial persuasion than Joe Mancuso. He is the founder of the world's largest nonprofit association of entrepreneurs, the Center for Entrepreneurial Management, Inc. (CEM), which has grown to a membership of approximately 3,500. He established eight CEO (Chief Executive Officers) Clubs around the country to provide a valuable forum for the incubation of ideas. Joe Mancuso's wealth of contacts and experience with CEM provide an excellent knowledge base from which he creates for his reader an atmosphere in which personal dreams and aspirations can become reality. The philosophies that he presents and develops in *Winning with the Power of Persuasion* offer insights into the win-win mentality.

Workshops and seminars around the world attempt to meet a growing public awareness and desire to develop and to refine personal goal setting. Joe Mancuso leads his reader on a step-by-step pathway to achieving those goals not only by well-established methods, which are often overlooked, but also by novel approaches, about which even the most experienced entrepreneur will wonder, "Why didn't I think of that?"

Joe Mancuso extols the mastermind concept in his book, in which knowledgeable and involved peers are used as sounding boards to explore ideas, opportunities and problems. He outlines the sequence that successful entrepreneurial persuaders use to gather information, seek advice and make decisions. He proves beyond a doubt that the mastermind philosophy is always more powerful than using a single brilliant mind to resolve multifaceted issues. This chapter alone would entice any would-be entrepreneur to buy the book.

To discover the natural *f*ear, *a*nxiety and *r*ejection (FAR) that reside deep within us, Joe Mancuso helps the reader to identify with the problems and the challenges met on a daily basis. He turns the FAR premise into page after page of insightful analysis of an entrepreneur's psyche and offers remedies for the FAR found in the reader's own life.

Also sprinkled throughout the book are amusing stories and poems that illustrate techniques for the reader to use in solving even the most unsolvable dilemmas in a relatively easy way. This book imparts the mystical touch of ancient Indian cultures to the movers and shakers in today's society. Mancuso draws not only on his own experiences but also on the experiences of those who are the recognized rainmakers. He examines the psyche of entrepreneurs, who at the very moment of conception of a movement or a trend will rush to fill a void and will create a new niche for themselves. Rainmakers are cutting-edge thinkers. They are able to spot trends and are part of the early group in any success. They make the success happen, not by watching, but by participating. Rainmakers are not necessarily smarter mentally but smarter at figuring out how to get an advantage. That difference can result in a downpour rather than a light drizzle.

Mancuso explores in-depth the varying characteristics inherent in typical entrepreneurs. He treats their drives and ambitions, their strengths and weaknesses, their triumphs and failures with equal consideration.

Mancuso relates stories of the rich and famous, and of the not-so-famous, to contrast the avenues that can be traveled. He acknowledges that each is a rainmaker. Most are able to create rain over a significant part of the world. Some are able to create thunderstorms, while others cause only showers.

You will discover that Joe Mancuso does not try to reinvent the wheel in this book. Instead, in his relaxed, easy manner, he sets in motion thought processes that spark the entrepreneur in each of us.

—Jim Miller
Miller Business Systems

Jim Miller's Million Dollar Certificate

One Million Dollar Certificate

Pay to:

The Sum of: *One Million Dollars - $1,000,000⁰⁰*

This is a guarantee to feel like **$1,000,000⁰⁰** if you do the following with your life:

1. Be Enthusiastic
2. Smile
3. Say "Thank You"
4. Be an Achiever
5. Be a WE Person and a TEAM Player

6. Listen and Communicate
7. Put in Extra Effort
8. Set Attainable Goals
9. Believe in Yourself
10. Say "TERRIFIC"

Jim Miller

Authorized Signature

NON-NEGOTIABLE

Copyright © All rights reserved.

Preface

This book focuses on how people are separated from their loose change by the most persuasive people in the world. These entrepreneurial persuaders can charm the pants off you and then get you to ask, politely, if they would do it again. And again.

These rainmakers are an antidote to the world's current economic crisis. While they seldom tell "all the truth and nothing but the truth," they do create jobs and wealth. Consequently, all societies, even on other continents, have a special fondness for these people. Jobs and economic growth are a worthwhile counterbalance to not telling all the truth all the time.

Entrepreneurs are the heroes of American society. They blossom in the American capitalist system like nowhere else in the world. They are legends in all countries and cultures. I have done entrepreneurship seminars in 40 countries around the world, and I can tell you that the American entrepreneurial persuader has no equal in any other culture. The world looks to Americans for this phenomenon.

The good news is that we grow them in abundance. The bad news is that not all of these creatures grown in the wild are nice, likeable or totally honest.

What I'm about to share has to do with how entrepreneurs persuade and what techniques they use to get a leg up and eventually succeed. Dancing around totem poles with long headdresses while chanting for rain isn't always easy. Gathering a long line of followers to join your efforts is even more difficult. But if you can do it long enough and not be accused of flim-flam, you can use magic and mirrors and mirages until it eventually rains. *You've got to fake it until you make it.*

Thank God for rain because it brings new life, new hope and prosperity. No position is more noble in a capitalistic system than the coveted title of rainmaker.

While all MBA programs now require an ethics course for graduation, the practices in the real world continue to be equal but opposite for academia. While students are studying being totally honest in the classroom, the books are being written about rainmakers. The promise of rain is very powerful.

Hence, this book has a touch of the conman, the P.T. Barnum sideshow and stories of the great entrepreneurs who create wealth and bring jobs. As Russia and Eastern Europe switch to a free market economy, they will learn the art of keeping chits, exchanging favors, negotiating for the fun of it and seeing double images. They will begin to understand why rainmakers need all that magic, those headdresses and the long dances and chants to make rain.

The concepts presented in this book were gathered by a participant/observation methodology over three decades. In America a unique breed of charismatic entrepreneurs exists who are able to persuade more easily than others. I claim to know more of these people on a one-to-one basis than anyone.

Entrepreneurial persuaders are all superior salespeople, negotiators and motivators. These *con*vincing folks generate numerous followers. They possess the power of the persuader with a purpose. They possess more power than the tribal chieftain because without rain there is no life. Chiefs come and go, but rainmakers survive through changing administrations.

In American culture, entrepreneurs are the cowboys of capitalism. They are the rock stars and the folk heroes of business. Notice that rainmakers rhymes with "movers and shakers." Both have the unique ability to make it happen, to do the impossible, to hit a home run in the ninth inning and win the game. How do they do it? Are they superhuman or just lucky? Are they using mirrors to create these illusions?

The answer is that they are more persuasive than professional managers or politicians or any other category of people.

They get people to believe in dreams, and their dreams often become reality. They are very powerful, and I will show you in this book how they do it. Not why—just how. Anyone can adopt these methods and principles. You need not be special to become an entrepreneurial persuader.

Persuasion appears in many forms. The entrepreneurial kind is used primarily by individuals who are convincing others to follow their dreams, to see their vision or to accept their solution.

There are other types of persuasion too, like coaching or coaxing someone to accept your view. These are less extreme and, therefore, less effective. However, if you are running a nonprofit social agency or a religious or educational institution, these other types may be more appropriate. The entrepreneurial persuader is at the extreme end of the economic persuasion spectrum.

This book explores the ways and means by which entrepreneurial persuaders achieve their objectives. They employ all of the nine persuasion approaches below to make it happen.

1. Assertiveness
    - Demand that a person do it.
    - The rules require a person to do it.
    - Remind the person of what to do.
2. Blocking
    - Threaten to stop working with the person.
    - Ignore the person and stop being friendly.
    - Engage in a work slowdown until the person does what you want.
3. Coalition
    - Obtain the support of coworkers to back up your request.
    - Make your request at a formal meeting where others will support you.
4. Exchange
    - Promise an exchange of favors.
    - Remind the person of past favors provided.
    - Keep chits on a scorecard.
5. Ingratiation
    - Be polite and humble while making the request.

- Be friendly and complimentary while making the request.
- Sympathize with a person about the hardships that a request will entail.

6. Rational Appeals
   - Write a detailed plan justifying a request.
   - Present numerical information and explain the reasons supporting your point of view.

7. Sanctions
   - Threaten to get the person fired.
   - Threaten to block a promotion.
   - Threaten to give an unfavorable performance evaluation.

8. Upward Appeal
   - Appeal to higher levels to intervene in support of your request.
   - Go with the person to see your superior.

9. Entrepreneurial Persuasion
   - All eight of the above.

This unique subset of the tiny universe of entrepreneurs does things that are unorthodox and sometimes crazy. Often this behavior crosses over the ethical lines. Sometimes getting the job done is not as important in the long term as being well liked. Sometimes, the task or mission gets in the way of being popular. *Entrepreneurial persuaders would rather beg for forgiveness than ask for permission.* I am a messenger, not an evangelist, and am therefore sharing my observations on how entrepreneurial persuaders get so many to do so much.

—Joe Mancuso
January 1993

1 *Entrepreneurial Persuaders*

Who Are the Rainmakers?

In the old tribal system, the rainmakers occupied a unique position of respect. Rain brings life for crops and animals and, in turn, prosperity for the people. So special are the rainmakers, even in African tribes of today, that tribes will often kill them before they are ready to die, as their death from natural causes could bring hardship to the tribe. The Banjar tribe in West Africa beats the rainmaker during droughts, and tribes in the upper Nile rip open the bellies of rainmakers to unleash the rains.

A little bit of the "con" is in every rainmaker who sells hope to the needy. This is an important quality because rainmakers must use entrepreneurial persuasion to survive. The good news is that it always rains eventually; the bad news is that occasionally it takes so long that no one can convince the tribe to be patient. That's when they need a new rainmaker. These are the folks I've unearthed in this book.

They are the kissing cousins to what Tom Wolfe in *The Bonfire of the Vanities* calls "Masters of the Universe," what Michael Lewis in *Liar's Poker* calls "Big Swinging Dicks" and what Ayn Rand in *Atlas Shrugged* calls "the Prime Mover," a phrase borrowed from Aristotle to mean God. I call them rainmakers. I hadn't heard of Anthony Bianco's book, *Rainmaker: The Saga of Jeff Beck, Wall Street Mad Dog*, until I finished this

1

book, but I was pleased to discover that Jeff Beck, the Wall Street wizard, fits my definition like a glove.

Have you ever invested in a small growing business? Have you ever been invited to invest money in an entrepreneurial venture? The people who do this professionally are called venture capitalists, and today there are fewer than 1,000 businesses in America with this purpose. But another group of people, a million times more in number, provide the seed capital to the majority of America's start-up companies. They are called "angels." Not the ones who live in heaven, but friends and relatives of the rainmakers who raise money.

When rainmakers get to be the size of Jeff Beck, Michael Milken or Ted Turner, they are just too complex to define. But even at an early age, they followed the persuader's first rule: Never cheat, lie or steal. The secret of success for a small business owner is to learn from the rainmakers how to win with the power of persuasion.

Aspiring Rainmakers

In the early 1970s, I was chairman of the management department of Worcester Polytechnic Institute (WPI) in Massachusetts. In my undergraduate course in entrepreneurship, we always took a field trip: We rented a bus and visited the state unemployment office, bankruptcy court and Haymarket Square in Boston. No one on the faculty or in the administration approved of this excursion, but I did it for seven years despite their resistance.

The trip to Haymarket Square was to buy fruit to be sold when we returned to campus. The students were divided into competitive teams. Each team had $50 to purchase food at this open-air market, and the winning team was the one that made the most money by following a one-page set of rules. Students acted as scorekeepers and monitors, and the competition was lively.

Some teams didn't make their $50 back and had to eat the remaining fruit over the next few days. Most teams at least doubled their money, and some made two or three times their investment. These students received As for this activity.

Here's what the rainmakers did. Some bought whole water-melons, or boxes of grapes or cantaloupes. Then they sold chances for 50 cents each to other students to buy the merchandise. At the end of the day, they drew the chances from a hat and passed out their winnings to their classmates. They made ten or twenty times their money. Other rainmakers used more than the allotted $50 to buy more fruit, or they used the extra outside money to hire salespeople to stir up activity at their fruit stand. One of the teams promised their friends that they'd wash and polish their cars if they bought from them. Really, the list is endless.

Do you see how they bend the rules? Do you see how they cheat a little and press the limits of the law? They believe that a white lie is better than a black one.

These college kids, and I've stayed in touch with a good many of them, were rainmakers ready to blossom. The college administration wanted to expel certain students. The faculty wanted me to flunk the ones who made too much money or ran lotteries. Other colleagues wanted several of the rainmakers to take the course a second time.

Not all entrepreneurs are crooks or cons, but most are not as nice as the late Sam Walton. The colorful founder of Wal-Mart received a $4 million advance for his life story. It's the largest ever for an autobiographical business book (Iacocca received only $150,000), and it's partially because there is a shortage of nice guys among the rainmakers.

The Best Rainmaker in the 1800s

I still haven't answered the question Who are the rainmakers? While I have avoided making a list of rainmakers or naming living entrepreneurs, one in history holds a special spot in my heart. He was one of the originals of this breed. Along with his rain came packets of wampum that he sprinkled liberally among the Indians while lining his own pockets with hard cash.

He was born in 1810, when America was composed of only 18 states. He died in 1891, at the age of 81, when there were 44 states. He operated in Bridgeport, Connecticut, a town that recently tried to go into Chapter Eleven bankruptcy. I asked a few

Bridgeport politicians whether the town was in bankruptcy, and they said they thought that the University of Bridgeport was bankrupt, but they were unsure about the town. Interesting place. (Bridgeport University was subsequently sold to Reverend Moon's Unification Church for about $50 million in May 1992.)

This man was the master of merriment and mischief, the person who said, "The bigger the humbug, the better." This showman smoked ten cigars a day, married a woman 40 years younger than he and left his name on the three-ring circus. P. T. Barnum liked to claim that he invented the audience and that he held patents on the process. But the 17 years ran out long ago.

Did you know that P. T. Barnum didn't get involved with the circus until he was 60 years old? Ray Kroc of McDonald's and Colonel Sanders of Kentucky Fried Chicken were also in their late fifties before they started creating rain. Yet these three old-timers accounted for more jobs than all the government programs to date!

P. T. was always pulling your leg to get at your wampum. His "humbugs" were so clever that people came back to see them again and again. For instance, instead of labeling the exits as "exits" he put up a sign saying "egress." That way, people would walk out to see the "egress exhibit" and have to pay again to reenter through the entrance. He was also a popular lecturer, and in one year alone, 1859, he gave the same seminar, "The Art of Money Losing," more than 100 times to some 3,000 people. He made money on losing money. He enjoyed pulling your leg, and he gets my vote as "The Rainmaker of the 1800s."

I hope this example helps you to understand the concept of the entrepreneurial persuader.

The Principles of Entrepreneurial Persuasion

Rainmakers use persuasion to seed the clouds and rain dances to release nature's forces. Persuasion is not intimidation or manipulation. It is a combination of selling, negotiating and motivating. The more complex phrase, "entrepreneurial persuasion," uses the adjective "entrepreneurial" to describe a kind of persuasion. You do not have to be an entrepreneur, owner or starter of a business to be an entrepreneurial persuader. You can simply use this form of persuasion as a means of achieving goals and surviving.

SPIA: Persuasion with a Purpose

An example of this form of persuasion is an approach I describe in Chapter 9. It's called SPIA, which stands for the *s*mallest *p*ossible *i*nherent *a*dvantage. It could also be simplified to NEER, *n*aturally *e*xisting *e*conomic *r*elationships. NEER is a combination of two principles:

- Plan your work and work your friends.
- Get the money and the hearts and minds will follow.

It's not quite as simple as that, but it's really not much more complex either.

When entrepreneurial persuaders need to accomplish a task, they first tackle the objectives that are easiest to conquer, thereby achieving small victories before moving on to more difficult tasks. That's why I call it the smallest possible inherent advantage. This is a very simple concept, but it is the heart and brains of the persuasive process. Smoke and mirrors may be the fingers and the toes, but SPIA is the vital organ of persuasion.

In Walter Hailey's example of persuasion, described in Chapter 3, you'll see that he once sold flour and subsequently returned to the flour distribution universe, from the grower to the grocer, to sell insurance. Again, it made sense because he had contacts there. He wasn't starting cold. He had an inherent advantage, so it was an easier sell. It was downhill.

For example, if you are selling laser printing services, an SPIA application—the way an entrepreneurial persuader would sell more laser printing services—is to find similar outlets. If you are currently selling laser printing to Merrill Lynch, doesn't it make sense that Oppenheimer (a competitor) might also need the same services? Or that Merrill Lynch's customers, suppliers or friends might benefit from this same service?

The same principle holds for other naturally existing relationships that are not economic. A nonprofit social agency could begin with naturally existing social relationships, or an educational institution might have naturally existing collegial relationships. Again, these are usually not as effective as economic relationships, but in the long run they may work better in those kinds of agencies.

Are rainmakers better persuaders than other types of people? Yes. Does this ability alone account for their power? No. Most of their persuasive power comes from the other aspects of their behavior. Their knowledge of the audience to be persuaded is one of those aspects. They understand the following basic principle of persuasion:

Situation 1: Audience predisposed to your position (favorable) } **One-sided argument**

Situation 2: Audience against your position (unfavorable) } **Two-sided argument**

The most popular example of this type of issue concerns convincing drivers to wear seat belts. A one-sided argument, such as seat belts save lives, is more convincing to people who already favor them. A two-sided argument, such as seat belts save lives even though they can be a bit uncomfortable while driving, is more persuasive for people who do not like to use them.

The message is simple. A good persuader learns the position of the audience before shaping his or her persuasive message. Rainmakers don't make scientific surveys; they know things intuitively. They know instinctively how to persuade. They won't waste a two-sided argument on an audience that is already predisposed to their position.

Why 90 Percent of People Fail To Reach Their Goals

In Walter Hailey's Power of Persuasion seminar, he states that his NEER system is the best way to achieve your goals. He claims that The Carnegie Institute of Technology analyzed the records of 10,000 people and concluded that 15 percent of success is due to technical training, brains and job skills, and 85 percent is due to personality factors and interpersonal skills.

When the Bureau of Vocational Guidance at Harvard University studied thousands of men and women who had been fired, they found that for every one person who lost his or her job for failure to do work, two people lost their jobs for failure to deal successfully with people.

The percentage ran even higher in a study reported by Dr. Albert Edward Wiggam in his syndicated column "Let's Explore Your Mind." Out of 4,000 people who lost their jobs in one year, only 10 percent lost out because they could not do the work. Ninety percent lost out because they had not developed the personality for dealing successfully with other people!

People buy not because they understand the product, but because you are enthusiastic about the product. *People don't care how much you know until they know how much you care.*

A Purpose Gives Meaning to Life

• •

"If a man hasn't discovered something that he will die for, he isn't fit to live."

MARTIN LUTHER KING, JR.

• •

When rainmakers have a purpose, their powerful force of persuasion can make the impossible possible!

Without direction, one's life has no meaning. The power of the persuader with a purpose—no matter what the purpose—makes life a celebration. All purposes work. Sure, this material is garnered from people with one common purpose, building businesses, but it applies to all purposes.

My father died on Christmas Eve in 1989, and two years later my mother said to me: "The hardest part of it all is that I have lost my purpose. You don't know how awful that is after 75 years with one." How often have you heard of two people who are intertwined of purpose dying at close to the same time? See how powerful purposes are?

A father's failure often spurs a son's success. Nobody knows that better than Leonard Abramson, 59, the feisty entrepreneur who has successfully launched three new businesses, including U.S. Healthcare, the $1.6 billion (1991 revenues) health maintenance organization.

Abramson's determination was fueled by his father's string of small business failures in and around Philadelphia in the 1950s. As a result, young Abramson had to take after-school jobs to bring home money for his mother. "Not too many people started out with less than I did," he says. That's an exaggeration, of course: Abramson never went hungry, but the humiliation he felt over his father's failures was as strong a goal as poverty, or stronger. To erase his father's imprint, "I felt I had to be successful," he adds. "I would *never* go bankrupt."

Pablo Picasso was one of the world's greatest entrepreneurs. He was so ingenuous that he never carried any cash with him. He paid for everything he needed with a check drawn on a bank account with only $100 on balance. When he bought groceries he paid by check, and when he took a limousine he paid by check. You see, no one ever cashed his checks because his autograph was usually worth more than the purchase. Picasso once said, "When I work, I relax: Doing nothing or entertaining visitors makes me tired."

Let me share something with you that I call the last 5 percent. Have you ever tried a recipe and found that it didn't taste right? Do you think the chef told you 100 percent or 95 percent of how to make it? Likewise, have you ever heard of someone who got a bank loan even though he was a poor credit risk? Then a few years later, you discovered that someone countersigned the loan. That's the last 5 percent. When it comes to persuasion, the last 5 percent comes from a purpose.

The Alarm Clock

The experience of a bachelor friend presently on his third business dramatizes the difficulties caused by a lack of purpose. In the mid-1960s, along with a college roommate, he started his first small company in the electronics industry. The two-man team built the company to a modest size and then sold it to a major electronics corporation.

Their initial capital was $3,000 each, and the company's sale returned them about $100,000 each. While building this initial company, they forfeited salaries, worked hard and long and made all the managerial mistakes. It was a typical first entrepreneurial experience—not a big success, not a big failure.

Bigger goals were on the horizon for the dynamic duo, for they hadn't realized the complete fulfillment of their impossible dream. Together they invested $100,000 each and began a new company. They had a purpose and a plan. Remember, a purpose comes before a plan.

This new company followed the same pattern as their first one, only this time they were more seasoned. And this time they made it big. My friend sold his share of the company about four years later at a very nice gain of several million dollars. His roommate stayed on to hold the company together.

Now the fun began. My friend was a bachelor in his early thirties, good-looking and rich with several million dollars in cash. Many people in this situation would have spent their time lounging on beaches, drinking scotch and playing tennis. Those things satisfied my friend for about six weeks. Somehow, he managed to stretch his period of idleness out to a year and a half, largely by indulging his whims.

For example, he and I went to a department store to do some shopping. He planned to buy everything of interest to him in the store—items that he had always wanted. He bought a color television, a stereo, a pair of walkie-talkies, a battery charger for his car, expensive clothes and a range of more frivolous items. One thing he had always wanted was a special AM-FM digital alarm clock radio, which also plugged into the coffeemaker and turned on the lights. It flashed the time on the ceiling, too. He bought it on sale for less than $100.

As he lived through this period of purposeless existence, he developed a guilt complex about doing nothing. After all, he reasoned (and rightly so), isn't every red-blooded American supposed to be working hard every day? Isn't that the American way?

One morning at seven o'clock, he reached over and grabbed his multipurpose alarm clock and threw it out his third-story window, coffeepot and all. That darn clock had kept waking him up at those ungodly morning hours, but it wasn't as sweet as the old $1.95 buzzer alarm that he carried in his suitcase when he was working. As he expressed it, "It was the most lonely moment of my life when I realized I had no place to get up and go to in the morning. I'd lost my purpose."

It seems a pity that those of us who are temperamentally suited to making a lot of money aren't able to adapt ourselves to enjoying it, while those of us who are psychologically suited to enjoying a lot of money aren't oriented toward making it!

Contrast this alarm clock story with the stated claim by the CEO of colorful Southwest Airlines, Herb Kelleher, that he works 365 days of the year. Is that a purpose? He says the speed of the leader is the speed of the pack. He likes to quote Napoleon: "He'd rather have an army of rabbits led by a lion than an army of lions led by a rabbit."

Bernard Loiseau, a chef at his restaurant in Saulieu, France, *Côte d'Or*, also works 365 days a year. He invested $5 million of borrowed money to turn his restaurant 150 miles south of Paris into a three-star rating in Michelin's guide. He has not taken a vacation in 16 years. Does that sound like a purpose?

Purposes are often developed early in life, usually during childhood. If you were poor as a child, you may seek to be rich as an adult. I don't know anybody who does this one in reverse order! Or if your parents didn't go to college, it can become *their* purpose to send you to college, or to make you a doctor or something like that. These purposes are like the Itsy Bitsy I describe in Chapter 2. In combination with persuasive techniques, they can shape your life and the lives of thousands of other people who associate with you.

As a child, when you have a quicksand foundation for a purpose, when you try to build on that foundation, it comes tumbling down. It is hard to tell the quicksand and the solid ground apart because from a distance they appear the same. Only when you start building on this childhood event does its true nature become apparent.

The Entrepreneur's Quiz

As founder of the world's largest nonprofit association of entrepreneurs, The Center for Entrepreneurial Management, Inc.

(CEM) and the Chief Executive Officers Clubs (CEO), as I mentioned earlier, I claim to know more entrepreneurs on a one-to-one basis than anyone I know. I have spent the last 15 years running this membership association. The prior 15 years were divided about evenly between being an entrepreneur who advised other entrepreneurs and being an academic who wrote about them.

About a quarter of a century ago, I first published a 25-question profile of this membership. I developed the data by surveying 3,000 individuals who paid $96 for annual dues. To some extent, that's what made this research unique—that these people voted with money to be classified as entrepreneurs.

This research was originally published as a diagnostic test to determine a person's entrepreneurial profile. In a self-grading system, participants could contrast their traits with the results of the survey. Eventually, this tool became popularly known as "The Entrepreneur's Quiz," and it has been updated every few years. For a current copy of this quiz, send $10 to: Joseph R. Mancuso, The Center for Entrepreneurial Management, 180 Varick St., New York, NY 10014, 212/633-0060, Fax 212/633-0063.

I discovered in my research that entrepreneurs share many common characteristics, too many to be merely coincidental. One may be a shy, gentle engineering student who turns her technical know-how into a gadget that helps the space shuttle fly more safely. Another could be a brash marketing major who hits on a better way to sell toothpaste. Despite their personality differences, these two persuaders often share many traits. By studying what entrepreneurs have in common, others can determine their own match of traits.

Here is a capsule of the classic traits of these "ready-fire-aim" types.

- *Entrepreneurs* are people who know a great deal about very little and who go along learning more and more about less and less until, finally, they know practically everything about nothing.
- *Persuaders* know very little about many things and keep learning less and less about more and more until they know practically nothing about everything.

- *Entrepreneurial persuaders* start out knowing everything about everything but, due to their association with entrepreneurs and persuaders, end up knowing nothing about anything.

Following is a breakdown of some of the data taken from the 3,000 members of The Center for Entrepreneurial Management—or what I call "The Entrepreneur's Quiz."

1. The entrepreneur's traits.
2. Learning close to home.
3. More school? Nah.
4. Lemonade! Lemonade!
5. Where do you fit in? The oldest child.
6. Money alone isn't enough.
7. Doer or thinker?
8. Flip again, double or nothing.
9. Love blooms around every corner.
10. Abdicate versus delegate.
11. A place for everything.
12. Is the glass half empty?
13. The competitive spirit.
14. Problem solving.
15. Risk taking.
16. The entrepreneurial perseverance rooster.
17. The shortcut.
18. What is an entrepreneur?

Let's analyze each point more closely.

The Entrepreneur's Traits

• •

"If you give a man a fish, you feed him for a day. If you teach a man to fish, you feed him for a life- time."

OLD PROVERB

• •

When Michael Dell was a 19-year-old freshman at the University of Texas in Austin, he raised a little cash by selling computer clones from his off-campus apartment. Business was so good that he didn't bother registering for his sophomore year courses.

Dell's lack of education hasn't hurt him, though. Sales at Dell Computer Corporation topped $500 million last year, and in an industry flush with entrepreneurial success stories, Dell ranks right up there with Bill Gates at Microsoft, Rod Canion at Compaq and Steve Jobs, the founder of Apple.

Creating a successful business from nothing requires motivation and perseverance that borders on obsession. Sometimes it demands ruthless behavior and a willingness to neglect everything but the business, including family and friends. Many successful entrepreneurs are considered antisocial, and some are thought of as downright nasty.

Learning Close to Home

The independent way of life isn't so much genetic as it is learned, and the first school for any entrepreneur is the home. If you have a parent who's self-employed, you're more likely to launch a business than if your folks are, say, civil servants. The parents of Ted Turner, Howard Hughes, Fred Smith and Donald Trump were self-employed, and studies show more than 60 percent of all successful entrepreneurs can claim at least one self-employed parent.

More School? Nah.

Many entrepreneurs are impertinent and boast an almost compulsive need to be right. Few teachers appreciate that attitude. That's why many entrepreneurs aren't college graduates, and only a precious few reach graduate school.

Failure is a part of this scenario. Entrepreneurs aren't known for their high grade point averages. Many receive failing grades at some point in their college careers, unless they were wise enough to drop the course when their interest waned. They may also have failed in past jobs where they weren't allowed to think for themselves. This was the reason Thomas Watson was fired in 1913 from National Cash Register Company (now NCR Corporation). He joined a competing tabulation and recording company and ended up running it for about 40 years. Then his son ran it for the next 16 years. He also changed its name to International Business Machines Corporation, and then to IBM.

There's a famous story told about Tom Watson. One of his subordinates made a horrendous mistake that cost the company $10 million. He was called into Watson's office and said, "I suppose you want my resignation." Watson looked at him and said, "Are you kidding? We just spent ten million dollars educating you."

Both founders of Apple Computers were college dropouts, too.

Hugh Hefner, the founder of *Playboy* magazine, left his job at *Esquire* because they refused to give him a five-dollar weekly raise.

But this is changing today as college degrees are easier to obtain. The newer entrepreneurs are probably college graduates, but they were seldom first in their class. We like to say that the A students go on to write books and be college professors, and the B students spend their life working for the C students.

Lemonade! Lemonade!

Most enterprising adults began as enterprising children. If you were an innovative kid who developed new ways to earn money, that entrepreneurial spirit will likely reemerge throughout your life. I am not just talking about the summer you mowed lawns for $5 each, or the paper route you held for three years. The real entrepreneurs of tomorrow promoted dances at the local community center and sold encyclopedias door to door. They sold the newspapers on the corner, or expanded a small home route system by selling the apartment houses.

They saw the potential income of shoveling snow on a winter day, but instead of putting on gloves and galoshes, they hired other kids to do the dirty work and handled the more sophisticated (and somewhat warmer) sales efforts.

Where Do You Fit In? The Oldest Child

If you're the oldest child in your family, the entrepreneurial world is your oyster. With an average of about 2.5 children per American family, the chances of being the first born are only 40 percent. Yet entrepreneurs tend to be the oldest children almost 70 percent of the time. One reason: The motivation to achieve is much higher among those born first, according to studies at Harvard and Columbia universities. That means if you're a second or third child—and there aren't at least six years between you and your next oldest sibling—you're bucking severe odds by trying to launch a business. While I have no data to prove it, I like to believe second children tend to be lawyers—those unlucky souls who spend their lives cleaning up the messes caused by their older siblings. Then they survive against the bigger and stronger older child by getting help from the laws established by their parents. "Mommy, do you know what Tommy did?"

Money Alone Isn't Enough

If your prime motivation for starting a new venture is to become rich, you probably won't succeed. Entrepreneurs start businesses because they can't stand working for someone else. They want to call all the shots, and more often than not, money is simply a by-product (albeit a welcome one) of their efforts. Some more noble purpose is always behind their need to make rain.

Doer or Thinker?

When faced with a difficult question, do you buckle down and concentrate on finding a solution? Or do you mull the question over while doing other things until an answer emerges? Entrepreneurs favor the latter approach. They see it as the difference between working harder and working smarter. Rather than force an answer, they allow the answer to suggest itself whenever possible. Some people may think this is abdicating or avoiding a decision, but it's not. Deadlines can certainly prompt a quicker response, but the solution will probably be better when it's allowed to bubble up rather than pop out. Because they are persuaders with a purpose, they work both hard and smart.

Flip Again, Double or Nothing

The typical entrepreneur might surprise you at the race track. Instead of wagering it all on a long shot, self-employed executives would more likely bet on the three-to-one favorite. In fact, few entrepreneurs are high risk takers. They tend to set realistic, achievable goals. And when they do take risks, they're realistic, calculated risks that depend more on their personal skills than on chance. If an entrepreneur found himself in Las Vegas with his last $10, chances are he'd make telephone calls in search of a financial backer.

Another example is Will Rogers' well-known story of a child locked in a windowless room that had two feet of horse manure on the floor. Once the child got over the initial shock, the little optimist started digging in the odoriferous stuff, muttering, "With all this manure there must be a pony somewhere." Entrepreneurs seek out opportunities—and when they do not exist, they create them. Entrepreneurism is a synonym for optimism.

I pass along this story as another example of entrepreneurial optimism. Recently, an entrepreneur managing a business in Florida stayed at my home over the weekend. After he showered and shaved in the morning, he took out a pair of dice from his pocket and rolled them a dozen times on the breakfast table before sitting down to eat. My family just watched as though it was some sort of religious ritual equivalent to saying grace. Finally, as he put the dice away, I blurted out, "What are you doing?" He was mildly amused when he matter-of-factly said, "I roll dice every day because I might be lucky and not know it."

Today may be your lucky day, so treat the day as though it is and it will be.

Love Blooms around Every Corner

One of the biggest weaknesses of entrepreneurs is their tendency to fall in love too easily. They go wild over new ideas, new machines, new contacts and potential new businesses, but these love affairs usually don't last long. The problem is that entrepreneurs lose their objectivity during the infatuation period. They refuse to listen to reason from friends and associates. But when the idea or product proves to be disappointing, they start looking eagerly for the next new "love" to come along. It's like a sudden summer shower.

Abdicate versus Delegate

Choosing a business partner or right-hand assistant is a critical task for would-be entrepreneurs (see Chapter 10). Many search for bright, energetic people much like themselves. That's their first mistake. Would you be happy or efficient as someone else's assistant?

Choosing someone bright but lazy is a smarter move. These people aren't out to prove themselves, so they won't butt heads with you at every turn. Unlike entrepreneurs, they're good at getting others to do their work. That's called delegating. Entrepreneurs are seldom good delegators. Rather, they choose to say, "When you finish this job, bring it back to me." That's called abdicating.

A Place for Everything

Organization is the key to an entrepreneur's success. In fact, it's the fundamental principle on which all new ventures are based. How entrepreneurs organize their days varies by person, but every entrepreneur has some system for coordinating tasks and appointments. One strategy is to keep a "to-do" list on your desk or in your pocket, crossing off tasks as you complete them and adding to the bottom as needed. Pocket calendars work just as well, and the gadgeteers love the vest-pocket computers.

If you're regularly late for appointments, you'll likely flop as the head of a company, even if you're the brains and motivation behind the company's product or service.

Is the Glass Half Empty?

Entrepreneurs are eternal optimists. They believe that with the right amount of time and money they can do anything. You

don't need faith to move a mountain if you have enough workers and machines. Many also believe chance plays a part in their
successes but that being in the right place at the right time is a
result of smart thinking and hard work, not chance alone.

To illustrate the plucky optimism of entrepreneurs, consider
the story of the midwestern shoe manufacturer who sent his
two sons to rural India to scout out new markets. One wired
back: "No point in staying on, no one here wears shoes." The
other son wired back, "Terrific opportunities here. Thousands
are without shoes." Guess which son eventually took over the
business?

Sometimes this optimism short-circuits realism. It creates
within the entrepreneurs a blowfish appearance. Even when an
outsider pricks the blowfish with a sharp object, it just puffs out
again. That's because the optimism never leaves them. Only the
outward appearance can be altered, not the stuff down deep.

The Competitive Spirit

The most famous quote attributed to legendary football
coach Vince Lombardi is, "Winning isn't everything, it's the
only thing." But a lesser-known quote of his that's closer to the
entrepreneurial philosophy is, "We didn't lose any games last
season, we just ran out of time twice."

Starting a business or new venture is a competitive game, and
new entrepreneurs have to be prepared to run out of time once
or twice before experiencing success. Henry Ford, Milton Her-
sey and Walt Disney all failed miserably in their first businesses.
With the right persuasive purpose, however, they each added a
few more minutes to the clock.

Problem Solving

Never approach entrepreneurial persuaders with a problem
because they have enough problems of their own. Always
approach them with an opportunity because they never have
enough opportunities. Rather than solve the problem and seek
to have yourself declared a genius, seek to *dis*solve the problem. Make it go away. The same net effect—the problem is gone
in both cases.

Risk Taking

I have never bet on a horse. I have never played a game of poker or craps for money. I have never bought a sweepstakes ticket or even a state lottery ticket. Do not take this to mean I am a prude when it comes to gambling. I have taken many sizeable gambles, just never any of the above. Because of my own peculiarity, I have been curious about the behavior other entrepreneurs would exhibit at a horse race. Would they bet on the twenty-to-one shots, the odds-on-favorite or some complicated versions of the daily double?

The answers were a bit surprising. Popular opinion guesses that entrepreneurs would be betting on the ten-to-one shot— you know, the chance to make a killing. They are dead wrong. On the other hand, they would not bet on the house favorite, either. The odds are too short.

Entrepreneurs seem to thrive on the three-to-one shot, something they feel to be exciting but realistic. Even when our discussions left the topic of horse racing, their attitudes remained the same. They played for the realistic but achievable odds. They set reasonable and obtainable objectives. The philosophy that holds at the track also holds in business. They prefer to bet on the three-to-one shot, but then to stand at the rail, shouting and yelling frantically for their horse to run faster. All the cheerleading helps; we all need someone to cheer us on.

This brings to mind the story of the blind entrepreneur who challenged champion golfer Lee Trevino to a game. The entrepreneur said, "I'll bet you $10,000 that I can win, but you have to let me choose the time and place." Trevino said, "You're crazy. You could never win against me; you're blind. However, for $10,000 you're on!" The man smiled and said, "Great, I'll meet you tonight at midnight at Pebble Beach!" The perfect long shot.

The Entrepreneurial Perseverance Rooster

• •

> *"Small business success comes from ninety-nine percent perspiration, not the one percent inspiration."*
>
> JOE MANCUSO

• •

Describing an entrepreneurial persuader is like trying to describe an elephant when you're standing up close. As you feel and touch the elephant, it's impossible to understand what you're feeling and touching. When you're able to stand back and observe the elephant in perspective, you discover that the big gray blob of matter is an elephant. Describing an entrepreneur by dissecting the various parts has the same limitation. I've discussed the entrepreneur's traits, personality, inner motivation, secret desires and individual characteristics, but the entrepreneur exists more for the value of the whole than the parts.

The following story captures the entrepreneurial persuader's spirit and makes it easier to visualize the whole person. The story concerns a farmer whose chickens are not laying eggs anymore. The farmer is disgusted, so he sends away his current crop of 42 roosters.

Then the farmer goes to market to buy a new batch of roosters to get his hens laying eggs once again. While the farmer is shopping at the market, a short, sneaky-looking fellow approaches him and says, "I hear you're looking for 42 roosters. I think you're crazy because over here in the corner I have a skinny little rooster, an entrepreneurial rooster. But this is not an average rooster. This one can keep your whole henhouse happy, and they'll be laying eggs again."

The farmer chuckled. "A rooster that size? Do you know how many hens I have?" The man offered a 30-day money-back guarantee, which convinced the farmer to give the rooster a try. Remember, when risk is zero, transactions happen and money flows.

A few days later, the farmer noticed, much to his surprise, that the chickens were all happy and laying eggs. He felt kind of proud of that skinny little fellow and mumbled to himself, "By golly, the rooster is doing the job." After the tenth day, the farmer again looked outside, and not only were the chickens happy and laying eggs, but he noticed that the ducks, which were loose in the pond next to the chicken coops, were also happy and laying eggs.

A smile beamed across the farmer's face and he muttered, "By heavens, that little rooster!" A few days later he noticed that not only were the ducks and chickens happy and laying eggs; his very tall ostriches were also happy and laying eggs! The farmer couldn't believe his eyes. This rooster had turned the tide. On the thirtieth day, he looked out of his bedroom window, but the rooster was nowhere in sight.

The farmer was deeply concerned, so, he went outside to look for the rooster. He noticed far off in the desert a cloud of dust in the sky, and he wondered what it could be. He hopped into his truck and drove toward the cloud. As he approached it, he saw a flock of vultures circling a limp object laying on the ground. It was the rooster. His feet were up, his tongue was out, and his head was to the side. He looked dead.

The farmer felt that the rooster's death was a tragedy and a waste of an unusual kind of drive and spirit. He also remembered that if he didn't get the rooster back in the required 30 days, he was going to lose his money-back guarantee. So he hopped out of the truck, went over the rooster and reached down to throw him onto the truck. Just as he reached down, the rooster turned his head, bit the farmer on the hand and said, "Shh! This is the only way you can get these vultures!"

Persuasion works best when combined with perseverance.

The Shortcut

I have refined my definition of an entrepreneur over the last 25 years—from "a person who organizes a business enterprise for continuing profit" to my current definition of "ready-fire-aim"—but I haven't been able to find a simple way to determine whether you are one. (If you can't spell it, that doesn't help because no one can.)

The admissions department at Worcester Polytechnic Institute (WPI) in Massachusetts developed a quick test to determine a freshman's likelihood of not flunking out of this small engineering school. Students who had a paper route as a kid for more than one year never dropped out of school. The admissions staff found this single fact a better predictor of staying power than the SAT scores or the person's high school class ranking.

In 1988, I hit upon the shortcut—the paper route equivalent to not flunking out of engineering school. It has not yet stood the test of time, but it looks promising. Here's my single foolproof test to discover whether you are an entrepreneur:

- *Entrepreneur as the driver*:* Gets in the car and drives off. While driving, he or she adjusts the radio, air conditioner, lights, seats, rear and side mirrors, and finally puts on the seat belt. All of this is done at some peril as the car approaches maximum speed.
- *Hired hand as the driver*: Adjusts the radio, air conditioner, lights, seats, mirrors and puts on the seat belt. Then starts the car and drives off.
- *Entrepreneur as the passenger*: As the chauffeur or spouse adjusts the steering wheel, seat, mirrors, air conditioning, seat belt and radio—the entrepreneur-passenger shouts out uncontrollably, "For God's sake, start the car!"

So far, it looks like my Rosetta Stone.

What Is an Entrepreneur?

1. In *Webster's Ninth New Collegiate Dictionary*, the entrepreneur is: "en-tre-pre-neur (F, fr. *entreprendre*, to undertake); one who organizes, manages and assumes the risks of a business or enterprise.
2. In *The Achieving Society*, by Dr. David McClelland (Halstead, 1976), the entrepreneur is defined as "someone who exercises some control over the means of production and produces more than he can consume in order to sell (or exchange) it for individual (or household) income."
3. In *The Organization Makers*, by O. Collins and W. Moore, the academic fathers of entrepreneurship, the entrepreneur is identified as "a person who has created out of nothing an ongoing enterprise."
4. To friends, the entrepreneur is the person who is feverishly writing during an airplane flight while his or her companions enjoy drinks, movies and games.

---

*They all own radar detectors, not to speed, but to "save hassling with bureaucracy."

5. An entrepreneur is someone who is confused when responding to the question, "Are you an entrepreneur, or are you unemployed?"
6. "Entrepreneurship is the most fun you can have with your clothes on!" (Sven Atterhead of Sweden, head of the School for Intrapreneurs)

Who Is an Entrepreneurial Persuader?

It would be nice to point to one famous person—Fred Smith of Federal Express, retired Lee Iacocca of Chrysler, Bill Gates at Microsoft, Steve Jobs, Ted Turner or T. Boone Pickens—and say, "There is a perfect example of an entrepreneurial persuader." Unfortunately, that's not possible. All of these CEOs undoubtedly use many of the entrepreneurial persuader's techniques, but no one person is significantly more effective than another.

All of the CEOs mentioned above are rainmakers, and most of them can create rain over a significant part of the world. At the age of 35, Bill Gates of Microsoft has a greater net worth than the GNP of the entire country of Nicaragua; he can create quite a thunderstorm. T. Boone Pickens has even made it rain in Japan. And Ted Turner has Saddam Hussein as a loyal viewer of his daily showers. But most rainmakers are not celebrities. They are well known only in a small circle. Often they make it rain only in certain neighborhoods, or on certain streets, or over certain houses. But they get you just as wet. I can state categorically, however, that no rainmaker can be found working for the registry of motor vehicles or the post office.

By studying the press generated by a few of the celebrity rainmakers we can gain insight into how these folks think.

"Profits, Dick Snyder's Ugly Word" was a cover page story in the Sunday *New York Times* business section on June 30, 1991. Richard E. Snyder is the CEO of Simon & Schuster. He took over a $70 million enterprise in 1975 and turned it into the world's largest publishing house with 1991 sales of close to $2 billion.

Snyder's division contributes more than one-third of Paramount Communications' sales and profits. Not bad for a boy from Brooklyn who began as a Simon & Schuster salesperson 30 years ago. In fact, Paramount's CEO and Snyder's boss, Marvin Davis, is another good example of an entrepreneurial persuader. But let me share some of the entrepreneurial qualities that have contributed to Snyder's incredible success.

One of the first things Mr. Snyder told Charles Hayward, president of his adult trade division since 1986, was, "Remember Charlie, you have got to be willing to lose a deal to make a deal. In other words, if you do not have the strength of mind to know when to walk away from a negotiation, you will never be a good negotiator or a successful publisher."

That reminds me of a statement by a lesser-known persuader. "If you don't miss about one in twenty airplane flights, you are getting to the airport too early." Does that shock you? That's about 5 percent of all your flights. Most people miss only one flight in a lifetime and talk about it forever.

People who are highly driven or who are persuaders with a purpose are constantly juggling the trade-off of output versus time. That's one of the ways they outproduce normal folks.

They are stronger of mind because they are stronger of purpose, and often stronger of body. The body houses the mind, so keeping the house in order makes all the things inside it better-performing and happier tenants.

As an aside, I should mention Robert Pritikin and the work of his Longevity Center in Santa Monica, California. He was a CEO Club speaker in 1990, and his message convinced me of the benefits of his unique low-fat approach. His books on health, diet and a longer life are excellent.

Dick Snyder works hard and expects more from himself than he does from his colleagues. In fact, drop by his office after 6:30 P.M., and Mr. Snyder is likely to be in the midst of a grinding 90-minute session on his Stairmaster. At the age of 58, he has just given up smoking because he has so much to accomplish yet and isn't ready to die.

Watching him at his 75-acre farm in upstate New York— leaping over fallen trees, running up stairs or driving a forehand into the corner of the tennis court, you'd see his untamed restlessness and determination.

According to Snyder in *The New York Times* article, people want to be able to trust their leader, and they want their leader to be "somebody with a drive and a focus that captures them. You can be 'one of the guys,' and should be out of decency. But you must also earn some awe."

"If you think I'm tough," Mr. Snyder has confided to his colleagues, "you should meet my boss [Marvin Davis]."

You can see from this why it is easy to love or hate an entrepreneurial persuader but almost impossible to feel neutral about them. Even legendary baseball coach Lee Durocher's famous quote, "Nice guys finish last," is just not strong enough to capture the power of the persuader with a purpose.

But the entrepreneurial persuader is not just a bad guy, either. The former head of Continental Airlines, Frank Lorenzo, was hailed in the press as a bad guy. He was an early user of Chapter Eleven bankruptcy to fight the unions at Continental and Eastern. (Now all the other airlines are trying to use it, too.) But Lorenzo could not sustain success, so his legacy has become more that of a bad guy than a superstar.

Herb Kelleher, the colorful entrepreneur-lawyer who runs that maverick airline, Southwest, also has a union, but he plays the role of clown and cheerleader to his 8,600 employees rather than union buster. He uses humor as a persuasive tool, and he is a winner who has succeeded where being a bad guy alone has produced losers.

Conclusion: Bainton's Tombstone

I'll close with a statement from Viatech CEO Donald Bainton to sum up the essential qualities of the entrepreneurial persuader.

In 1983, Don Bainton retired as president of the Fortune 500 Continental Can Company. He became CEO of Viatech, which was at the time an engineering company with an annual revenue of just under $6 million. In 1992, Viatech expected to ship $300 million on a profitable basis. This is what Bainton wants written on his tombstone:

Relative intelligence: strategic and new product vision; results orientation; sensitivity to the arts and entertainment fields; impatience with lack of results or achievement of goals; intolerance of noncommitted, incompetent, bureaucratic or "political" managers; dislike of formal procedures, large or-

ganizations, bureaucracy and favorites. In my spare time, I enjoy many areas of interest and a diverse group of friends. However, in business, I am very demanding and insist that my colleagues are extremely capable, enjoy hard work and achieve results and objectives.

In summary, I've always been a results-oriented manager, giving rewards to those who achieve good results and meet objectives and conversely, removing managers who do not meet results and objectives. This very direct approach has consistently created very strong management teams in all of the entities that I have been associated with. However, it is not a "popular" method of management except for those who are capable of meeting results and objectives, and who will devote the time and effort necessary to achieve those goals. Those managers who are comfortable with that style of management have been loyal and strong members of our management groups. Many, if not most, of the managers who I have had to move, demote or discharge not only disagreed with this philosophy of management, but undoubtedly took it personally rather than as a reflection of a basic business strategy. In addition, I would like to think that my business actions were tempered by sensitivity and compassion for individuals where warranted.

It is my belief that if all businesses were run with a basic results-oriented philosophy, with rewards going to those who achieve results and objectives, not only would our business competitiveness improve, compared with countries like Japan and Germany, but our overall national productivity and balance of payments would be significantly improved. (Reprinted with permission.)

I have never met Donald Bainton, and I do not know anyone from his company. Like most rainmakers, he is not well known outside of business circles. Yet I feel as though I've met him a thousand times.

2 Overcoming Fear, Anxiety and Rejection

"There is no likelihood man can ever tap the power of the atom."

ROBERT MILLIKEN, NOBEL PRIZE IN PHYSICS, 1920

Itsy Bitsy

Walter Hailey is the only child of hard-working parents who lived on a small farm in the town of Mesquite, Texas. Hailey was smaller than most boys; in fact, he was so small he was known as "Bitsy," an outgrowth of a nickname given to him by his loving parents, Floyd and Betsy.

Hailey has turned Bitsy into an asset. The man is blessed with the unique ability to turn minuses into pluses and disadvantages into advantages. He doesn't eat lemons, so I don't know if he makes lemonade.

When his classmates gathered after school for sandlot football, the two team captains took turns picking players for their respective teams. Here is how Hailey recalls those frustrating times.

"A captain would pick a player for his team, then the other captain would make his selection. After all the boys had been picked, I was the last one standing there without a team. One of the captains would say to the other, 'Okay, you can have Bitsy.' And the other would respond, 'No, you can take him.' So there I was, a liability named Bitsy; someone nobody wanted on their team."

These deep-seated insecurities stuck in his memory and were vividly recalled as he grew into adulthood and found himself in the grown-up world of competitive business. It's often the deep-rooted insecurities in growing up that create the needs and desires and purposes in later life for a persuader.

"We all have a Bitsy in us," says Hailey. Everyone has insecurities dating back to their childhood years. Maybe you weren't the smallest kid in the neighborhood, but if you are honest with yourself, you'll remember disappointment and frustration even if you were the biggest kid on the block. Hailey believes successful people are those who have learned to deal with the Bitsies of their past. They have found ways of compensating for those early frustrations and insecurities.

Walter Hailey sometimes stands on a chair when he delivers a speech. He opens his speeches by saying, "I used to be six feet tall. That's before I got into selling. . . ."

Winners Overcome Fear, Anxiety and Rejection

• •

"Excessive fear is always powerless."

AESCHYLUS, THE SUPPLIANT MAIDENS, *463 B.C.*

• •

Walter Hailey built the Lone Star Insurance Company and sold it for $78 million before he became an evangelist for his Power of Persuasion seminar. He traveled with me as a speaker to all the CEO Clubs. Many of our members also attended a weekend bootcamp held at his home in the hills of Hunt, Texas. Here the concept of winners and FAR crystallized for me.

How does FAR happen? It's usually based upon childhood experiences, just like Walter Hailey's Itsy Bitsy. It's hard to develop confidence when you are young because life is bigger than you and you experience lots of setbacks. It's what creates FAR in our later lives.

Winners are individuals who took the problems and setbacks of childhood and turned them around to overcome *f*ear, *a*nxiety and *r*ejection. Walter Hailey is a winner.

My Version of Itsy Bitsy

Although I have written 18 books and untold articles and a monthly newsletter for 15 years, I have never told the following story.

It happened when I was in tenth grade. I transferred from Burr Junior High School to Bulkeley High School in Hartford, Connecticut, where the big kids went to school.

During the first month in this huge school—3,000 students compared to Burr's 400—I was required to sit in the temporarily erected bleachers on the stage of the massive auditorium. The Honor Society had to wear suits and ties and sit on the stage for one hour during the first period of school. The group of about 200 of us didn't have to do anything. Just sit in front of 3,000 kids.

I arrived at school a little early that day, wearing my only suit. It didn't fit, but I didn't know it. The Honor Society was all seated and quiet in the bleachers behind the curtain well before the 8:30 a.m. opening. I had a nice view and was looking forward to the one-hour session as a break from school work. None of the other kids could tell my suit didn't fit well because I was sitting down.

I had just had the devastating experience of having to start wearing both teeth braces and eyeglasses a few months earlier. I also had teenage acne. That was me: pimples, braces, four eyes and an ill-fitting suit. A real stud!

At about 8:15 a.m., the vice principal came over to me and said the student who was to read the one-paragraph cafeteria report had called in sick, and he asked me to read it for him. I looked it over, and there were only six sentences about how many spoons and forks had been lost last year. Duck soup for an honor student. It was my first chance to shine in front of the entire student body, of which at least half were available, older girls, so I agreed to do it.

I read and reread the page and was ready to go when the curtain rose. I was on my way to fame and glory. While awaiting my turn to perform, I toyed with the idea of leaving my new glasses behind. Even at this tender age, I understood the concept of "highest and best use." From that distance, the girls wouldn't be able to see the pimples or the braces, but the glasses could be seen all the way in the back row.

When my cue was given, I left the glasses on my seat and sashayed to the podium. It was to be my first public speech, and it was a big moment for me. I read the first sentence flawlessly into the microphone. I had it memorized, and I had a natural speaking voice. Zig Ziglar, old friend, if you are reading this, I even popped my p's and did you proud. Only five sentences to go to fame and glory! And maybe a new girlfriend. Then the problems began.

I couldn't find my place on the sheet of paper, and I couldn't read the words without my glasses. A few kids in the front rows started to giggle. When I brought the paper from the podium to my face, the rest of the kids started to laugh. I still couldn't find my place, so I turned on the podium light. The light didn't help at all, and by now the kids were shouting and cheering. So I put the paper on the podium and just gave up. The noise from the audience was deafening, and I froze.

The vice principal was seated on the stage behind me, but he was laughing so hard he was paralyzed to help a ninth grader.

Thank God for the math teacher (they are not all bad). She strode from the rear of the massive auditorium, down the center aisle, over to the side stairs, and up to the stage and over to the podium. She led me off the stage to a thunderous ovation. I was the most-liked clown in the school. Everyone knew who I was.

I went straight to the nurse and vomited until my mother took me home. I did not return to school for two weeks during which time I traded in those ugly glasses for contact lenses.

Today I make a good portion of my income as a public speaker. I'm so good at it that I have to turn down most dates. I've been doing it for several decades, and I've totally forgotten why I needed to become a public speaker. Why take the risk of another life-threatening experience?

These childhood experiences often form the basis for major life choices, sometimes subconsciously. They are the fire in the belly that drives the engine. They make the rainmakers. They provide our purposes, and you should appreciate all your little childhood setbacks. They made you what you are today!

• •

"We are more often frightened than hurt: Our troubles spring more often from fancy than reality."

SENECA, LETTERS TO LUCILIUS

• •

I had another childhood experience that caused me to be a writer but I didn't connect it until I was in my late thirties. So don't write off this concept just because the cause and effect are not readily apparent.

I never attended an English class during my four years in high school. I was an A student, and I was awarded the chance to work in the cafeteria. Both English and lunch alternated during the middle period of the day. If you worked one period, you got a free lunch. If you worked both periods, you also earned money. I got money and lunch and skipped all my English classes. After all, I reasoned, I knew that subject cold.

Because I couldn't read or write English, I chose to go to an engineering school. After graduating as an electrical engineer, I went on to get an MBA from the Harvard Business School. They didn't require much writing or reading skills either, so I was still safe. At Harvard all you needed was a good tongue.

After the Harvard MBA, I worked for seven years as a small business consultant along Route 128's golden corridor in Boston. My sales pitch to the 300-plus clients was always the same: "I don't write reports." In fact, I really couldn't write at all. I read only average, but a two-page letter took an hour.

When I hit 30 years of age, I started to worry. Then I realized that I couldn't write because I had never written anything. That year, I went to a high school bookstore and bought all the English books for grades nine through twelve.

Over the next 20 years, I wrote one major book a year. The one you are reading is my nineteenth. I've also published articles in the *Harvard Business Review*, the *Journal of Small Business*, the *Journal of Marketing*, and *Penthouse* and *Playboy*. All this from an engineer who can't spell "entrepreneur."

The Story of Tom: A Victory over FAR

• •

"Of all the passions, fear weakens judgment most."

CARDINAL DE RETZ, MEMOIRES, *1718*

• •

Recently, a friend called me from Wichita, Kansas, and asked me to counsel a 19-year-old family friend, Tom. His parents, whom I had never met, were prominent entrepreneurs in town and were desperate for help for their only child. He was failing in school and sports, especially basketball, and had no purpose in life.

I spent half a day with Tom and uncovered the cause of his problem. His parents divorced when he was seven, and over the next four years he lived with one then the other and then with both sets of grandparents. His parents remained business partners after the divorce. As luck would have it, they eventually remarried, and Tom returned to the family home just as he was entering puberty.

However, his parents divorced again, and Tom tightened up considerably when he mentioned this. The story had been pretty big news in Kansas. "Everybody in Topeka even knew about the comedy," he said, and shook his head.

So, his parents on that day were business partners, but each was married to someone else. Tom had reasoned that his grades in school and his inability to "put the ball in the hole" were directly related to this problem.

I could see he wanted sympathy for his confused upbringing. Everyone else had always responded to him with "Oh, you poor boy," and the real culprits of this were the two sets of grandparents who continued to echo the "poor boy" chant. It was his version of Itsy Bitsy.

I don't know what prompted my response, but it came spontaneously. I said: "You lucky man. You could be on your way to greatness. Did you know that most of the great people in history had troubled childhoods? Abraham Lincoln's mother was sent to a mental hospital, and Winston Churchill's should have been. This is true of most famous public and political figures."

Then I mentioned Picasso, Rembrandt, Matisse and a few other great artists. They had monumental family problems to overcome, I told him. The greatest artist in my view was Vincent Van Gogh, who suffered from porphyria (like epilepsy) throughout his life. Many say this debilitating disease is what gave him that famous penchant for brilliant colors, especially brilliant yellows.

"Did you know that Ted Turner's dad committed suicide?" I asked. "Or that Fred Smith of Federal Express was bedridden for a couple of years as a young boy?" I added: "Did you know that many famous entrepreneurs had devastating fights with one or both of their parents, and that many famous entrepreneurs were created by fathers who deserted the family? They had to fend for themselves or die."

After our discussion we went to the telescope fixed on the Manhattan General Post Office. Tom looked through the telescope as I said to him: "If you want a career at the post office, you need a nice, balanced childhood like the ones you read about in storybooks. If you don't believe me, walk over there and ask the thousands of employees a little about their background. I'll bet you not one of these postal employees is an offspring of an entrepreneurial couple who were married and divorced twice."

Tom recognized something positive in what I said and something positive in his parents and in his childhood. My message had reached the back of his brain.

After he left my office, I turned to my wife and said what was really on my mind: "Boy! You should have met this sweet young man from the Midwest. He's had it real tough. The poor kid is confused, and I can't blame him—his folks are more immature than he is. I doubt whether I could have succeeded with that kind of upbringing."

I eventually heard from a mutual friend that Tom had started a business and had a wedding planned later this year. I think I got to him.

Kids can do amazing things, if they have amazing things to do. But watch out for the five p's that can muck up a kid: parents, peers, preachers, professors and politicians. They produce pitfalls, perils and problems. What a kid really needs are possibilities.

According to Walter Hailey, the best antidote for an overdose of the five p's is reading aloud with your child this statement at bedtime every night:

"I promise I will never allow another human being to think less of me. I'm OK and you're OK."

"I always do what I ought to do when I ought to do it, whether I want to or not. No excuses."

My Favorite Entrepreneur: Fred Smith

As the founder and president of CEM and the CEO Clubs, I've gotten to know more entrepreneurs than anyone I know. And as I travel around the United States, people always ask me who I think is the greatest entrepreneur of all.

Instead of trying to rank the best of the best, I prefer to name my *favorite* entrepreneur: Frederick W. Smith, founder, chief executive and chairman of the Federal Express Corporation. (The runner up is H. Ross Perot.)

Smith is my favorite entrepreneur for ten reasons:

1. Smith was not a high-tech genius. And although the concept of delivering packages overnight was a great idea, it wasn't a new one; it took Fred Smith to make it work.
2. He didn't have an MBA or an engineering degree. He was an ex-marine who had flown reconnaissance missions in Vietnam before starting Federal Express. (No doubt this experience was valuable training for the ordeal of raising venture capital).
3. Federal Express started with just a business plan and raised more money than any previous company from the hard-nosed venture capital community.
4. In the early days, Smith ran out of money all the time, including his own personal fortune of several million dollars. It seemed as if he sometimes made payroll on little more than a prayer; in fact, legend says he once

won enough gambling in Las Vegas to make a payroll. I like that.

5. He never thought of quitting. This is my best reason for liking him.

6. He has run Federal Express from the beginning. And somehow he has successfully made the transition from entrepreneur to professional manager.

7. Before Federal Express, air express meant piggybacking packages on commercial airlines, which wasn't always a reliable method of delivering packages. Smith devised a way to serve that need. The idea of flying all packages to a central location (Memphis, Tennessee) for sorting and then rerouting to their final destination is a brilliant spoke-and-hub concept. Smith clearly showed the wisdom of shipping a package originating in Newark through Memphis, on the way to its final destination in New York City. I like brilliant ideas that sound stupid.

8. Building an idea into a $9 billion business is the mark of an inspired entrepreneur *and* manager. Although this feat is often referred to as the "impossible transition," Smith told the CEO Club of New York that being a successful entrepreneur and a successful professional manager are not mutually exclusive talents. "It's like being a great runner and speaking a foreign language," he said. "There's no reason one person can't do both."

9. The Federal Express concept was conceived from a term paper while Smith was an undergraduate at Yale University. His professor gave him C for the project. I'd like to see all the As in *that* class!

10. While addressing the CEO Club of New York, Smith relished the now-famous story of the C term paper. But he also confided he was so pleased with the grade on this paper that he rushed to call home, bragging, "I've gotten my second C at Yale, and now I'm on my way! I think I'll graduate."

Sure, you could say Fred Smith was a rich kid who parlayed a small fortune into a large one. And many people feel that way. "If I had several million dollars I could have done it too" is one common sentiment. But it's the commitment to invest every penny of your fortune in an idea regardless of whether it is $100 or $100 million.

It's the old ham-and-eggs breakfast story. You know, the chicken makes a contribution, but the pig makes a commitment. How many times have you heard someone say, "Do you know how to make a small fortune?" When you say no, they smile and deliver the punch line: "Start with a big one and then invest in a small, growing business." Smith made a commitment to make Federal Express succeed, and he did what he had to to make this commitment and his dream come true. That's why he is my favorite.

Selling an Idea

In the end, Smith was not out to make money. He already had wealth. He was out to make his dream come true. He wanted to prove the wisdom of his new package delivery system and his daring airplane schedules. He was a pilot who wanted to own and create an airplane business for profit.

At first he thought the government's Federal Reserve Bank would like the quick delivery concept of Federal Express enough to give his fledgling company a lot of business. He reasoned that a quicker method of delivering Federal Reserve checks would appeal to the banking system. He justified the quick delivery of checks by showing how much one day's float within the Federal Reserve banking system was worth. And then he showed that his system saved money for everyone.

It was perfectly logical, he reasoned—and that's why he named his company *Federal* Express. But he was wrong. The Federal Reserve System trades checks among each of its separately managed districts. And without unanimous cooperation from all districts (which he could not obtain), the idea wouldn't work.

But that didn't stop him. It only made him work harder at refocusing his business to save the company. He never considered quitting as an option. And that's why, when all is weighed, he is my favorite entrepreneur.

Smith reminds me of the world's first entrepreneur: the crazy guy who sold a business plan (actually a map) to a very rich Spanish lady (the Queen, naturally). He told her that if she'd give him three ships, he'd sail to China and bring back lots of gold. He was wrong, too, but as luck would have it, Christopher Columbus turned the world around with his "plan" map. And the world's first winner in the venture capital game was a woman.

This redheaded, freckle-faced Italian entrepreneur was born in 1451 and sailed east at the age of 41. After being turned down by King John of Portugal, he sold his concept to Queen Isabella of Spain. King Ferdinand went along with his wife's plan to sail east to reach the Indies to bring back the gold but never really trusted the Italians.

When he reached San Salvadore, Columbus called the inhabitants Indians because he really believed his business plan.

As with all "cons," this Italian rainmaker used to "fudge" the numbers in his ship's log to keep the 90 men on his three ships believing they were almost there. Columbus successfully convinced his shareholders and employees to believe in him as he became the first person to raise money based upon a written business plan.

Raising Money

. . . .

"Would you persuade, speak of interest, not of reason."

BENJAMIN FRANKLIN, POOR RICHARD'S ALMANAC

. . . .

The venture capital industry probably would not have flourished if Smith had not been successful with Federal Express.

Where other companies have made more money or made greater percentage returns for their investors, Federal had the unique advantage of having more venture capital investors in the deal than any other company at that time. In other words, Smith, as the Pied Piper (an entrepreneurial persuader), attracted a long line of followers.

The only thing wrong with Smith's spoke-and-hub delivery system is that it takes about $100 million to execute it. You have to own airplanes, a hub and a lot of trucks, and you have to employ a lot of people. If you do not treat the whole country as a single system, you lose the advantage of national advertising. So to pull off the Federal Express concept, Smith had to convince a lot of people of the value of his vision, because someone would surely ask: "Why can't we do it for ten million dollars?"

He knew the first person he tried to sell the concept to would be the hardest. He spoke with confidence to everyone, saying "Do you see the power, the beauty and the simplicity of what I'm trying to do? Do you think Federal Express will make a lot of money for a lot of people?" And when they answered yes, he then said: "You're not alone in your thinking. We now have the entire placement oversubscribed, and we are proud of that. However, if you are still interested in getting involved, why don't you come to the closing in case someone drops out or is unable to make it? Maybe at the last minute I could squeeze you into the placement."

Eventually, one hundred separate entities placed a million dollars each into Federal Express, and the question you have to ask yourself is, How many of those people did Fred Smith tell that story to?

In essence, it's a lot easier to sell the last million than it is the first million. Entrepreneurial persuaders know that.

The Rainmaker of the 1990s

Ted Turner, who gets pounded in the press as the mouth of the south and a flamboyant playboy, is a fine person and an independent thinker.

He was named *Time* magazine's Man of the Year in 1991. The honor came to him at the age of 53, the same age that his beloved father (and Turner did love him) shot himself in the head. The centerfold picture in *Time* shows Turner standing at his desk with his famous quotation displayed prominently: "Lead, follow or get out of the way." It's no accident that Ted's baseball team is called the Atlanta Braves.

When Turner addressed the CEO Clubs, he walked alone into the packed room at the Harvard Club. He walked up to me, and instead of saying hello and extending his hand, he asked me, "Where does the money go for this lunch?" I wasn't ready for that question, but I said "Nowhere. It stops right here." Turner didn't hear my answer as he was already starting to shake hands with the guests. He didn't really care what the answer was as long as there was one. If I had stuttered or asked him to repeat the question, I might have disappointed 350 CEOs who howled at his talk.

His two best lines were:

- "Early to bed, early to rise, work like hell and advertise."
- "Life is like a grade B movie. It's not so bad you want to walk out, but I don't know if I'd want to see it again."

He brought down the house, and he did it for free. No airplane fare, no fee, just because he liked what we were doing. He is truly an independent thinker and a class act—my choice for Rainmaker of the Decade.

3 *Creating Leverage*

"Heavier-than-air flying machines are impossible."

LORD KELVIN, PRESIDENT, ROYAL SOCIETY, 1895

Most new ideas are a repackaging of parts of old ideas, taking a bit from each to form a totally new concept. This book is an example of that process. The good material on the subject of negotiation, motivation and selling is combined to create a unique fourth subject: persuasion. In fact, many of these ideas may be so old that rereading them here may be nothing more than remembering what you have forgotten. But that makes it new, too.

selling ——— motivation ——— negotiation

PERSUASION

The Art of War*

> •
>
> *"The best soldier does not attack. The superior fighter succeeds without violence. The greatest conqueror wins without a struggle. The most successful manager leads without dictating. This is called intelligent nonaggressiveness. This is called mastery of men."*
>
> LAO-TSU, TAO THE KING
>
> •

Most of us think of settling a dispute as something akin to verbal boxing. You pound through your arguments until you get what you want. Much more elegant and effective models are the Oriental martial arts, such as aikido and t'ai chi. There, the goal is not to overcome force, but to redirect it—not to meet force with force, but to align yourself with the force directed at you and guide it in a new direction.

The best book of strategy was compiled more than 2,000 years ago by a mysterious Chinese warrior-philosopher, Sun Tzu. It's called *The Art of War*, and it has been eagerly adopted by modern military strategists, including Desert Storm General Norman Schwarzkopf.

Some see in the successes of postwar Japan an illustration of Sun Tzu's classic dictum, "To win without fighting is best." Here is a sample of some of his other philosophies:

- "All warfare is based on deception."
- "Offer the enemy a bait to lure him; feign disorder and strike him."

---

*Author Michael Crichton dedicates his best-selling book, *Rising Sun*, to the Japanese motto, "Business is war." Throughout the book, he claims that the normal way of doing business Japanese-style is through subterfuge.

- "In war, numbers alone confer no advantage. Do not advance relying on sheer military power."
- "The enemy must not know where I intend to give battle. For if he does not know where I intend to give battle, he must prepare in a great many places. And when he prepares in a great many places, those I have to fight in any one place will be few."
- "For to win 100 victories in 100 battles is not the acme of skill. To subdue the enemy without fighting is the acme of skill."
- "Thus, what is of supreme importance in war is to attack the enemy's strategy . . . "

Attila the Hun

Centuries ago, Attila shaped an aimless hoard of mercenary tribal nomads into the undisputed rulers of the ancient world. Attila, king of the Huns, was born in a chariot somewhere in the valley of the Danube River around the year A.D. 395. He was the son of King Mundzuk and could trace his ancestry for some 32 generations. When he became king, he controlled an army of 700,000 warriors, mostly barbarians.

Attila's legacy is not as well known to the Western world as that of Alexander the Great, Caesar or even Ivan the Terrible. But his legacy was that of a mighty king whose goodness and wisdom had no equal. His story is told in detail in a little book by Wess Roberts titled *The Leadership Secrets of Attila the Hun* (Warner, 1985).

America's most outspoken and visible entrepreneur, H. Ross Perot, of EDS and former presidential candidate fame, angered his boss, General Motors chairman Roger Smith, by trying to give out 500 copies of these leadership secrets at a dinner attended by the managers of GM's new Saturn division. Smith had fits when Perot sold EDS for $750 million to General Motors. Ross was eventually fired by Smith, and he loved it. Maybe you should emulate both Perot and Attila.

Machiavelli

More than 400 years ago, a Florentine statesman named Machiavelli wrote a book called *The Prince*, in which he set down the rules of politics. Machiavelli's work (which sprang up at a time when democracy was not in vogue) is often viewed as a blueprint for dictators, but *The Prince* is much more than that. The modern-day persuader can find plenty that applies to managing a business in Machiavelli's insights.

A Machiavelli sampler:

- "The first impression that one gets of a ruler and of his brains is from seeing the men he has about him."
- "A prince need trouble little about conspiracies when the people are well disposed, but when they are hostile and hold him in hatred, then he must fear everything and everybody."
- "A prince must show himself a lover of merit, give preferment to the able and honor those who excel in every art."
- "A man who wishes to make a profession of goodness in everything must necessarily come to grief among so many who are not good. Therefore, it is necessary to learn how not to be good, and to use this knowledge and not use it, according to the necessity of the case."
- "There is no other way of guarding oneself against flattery than by letting men understand that they will not offend you by speaking the truth."

Where Is Your Fulcrum?

Another age-old concept that has applications to modern business is leverage, discovered by Archimedes. His work ultimately led to the leveraged buyout (LBO) craze, which led to the junk bond market, which in turn contributed to the $500 billion savings and loan bail out. Drexel Burnham Lambert and Michael Milken are just following the law developed centuries ago among the Greek philosophers.

Figure 3.1   Two Ways To Increase Leverage

1. Lengthen lever.

2. Move fulcrum closer to object.

Archimedes once said, "if you give me a lever long enough and allow me to stand on the other side of the moon, I could use the lever to move the Earth." He was technically right. If you have enough leverage, you can do anything—even move the Earth.

Basically, you have two ways to increase your leverage: Either lengthen your lever or move your fulcrum closer to the object you want to move (see Figure 3.1).

The Science of Selling (SOS)

Walter Hailey understood the value of leverage when he worked as an insurance salesperson in the 1950s. "I really did well during those early days," he said. "I sold. I mean, I sold a whole lot. I sold my home, my car. I sold!. . ."

Like most rookie insurance people, he had his share of frustrations and disappointments. While the insurance business is highly profitable for some, most new salespeople find it is a tough way to make a living. Prospecting for new clients is the number one challenge for the neophyte insurance agent. It was no different for the wily Walter Hailey:

"I needed to find a way to overcome the Bitsy in me. I knew I had a lot of handicaps, and being the shortest guy around was just one of those disadvantages. There really wasn't any reason why a person should buy insurance from me instead of the next guy who is probably taller, better looking, smarter and better connected. This is when I hit on the idea of SOS—Science of Selling. I had to develop some high-tech ways of prospecting, and I had to find new and better ways of selling more policies in less time. Otherwise, how was I going to be a top producer? And I knew enough about the business to know that in commission selling, you have to sell more to earn more. Yet, I had only 24 hours a day to get it done. There had to be a better way to sell more and larger policies each day, or I wasn't going to earn the kind of money I wanted."

He was looking for a way to lengthen his lever to create leverage. Although Hailey is now in his sixties, I don't think he ever met Archimedes.

The Multiplication Factor

Hailey soon hit on what he calls the x, or multiplication, factor. It works like this: If you start with ten for a total of six times, you have the sum of sixty. But if you can substitute the pluses with the x factor, you end up with one million instead of only sixty.

$$10 + 10 + 10 + 10 + 10 + 10 = 60$$
versus
$$10 \times 10 \times 10 \times 10 \times 10 \times 10 = 1,000,000$$

The x factor is so simple that it tends to insult the intelligence of most attendees at Hailey's Power of Persuasion seminars. But it is a basic premise on which many of his formulas for success are built. If you can multiply your efforts and your energy instead of merely adding, the results can be staggering.

Hailey says he hit on the x factor when he decided to find ways of applying leverage to selling. It's another offshoot of an old truth, and it can trace its roots back to Archimedes.

· ·

"The intelligent know everything. The rich know everybody."

UNKNOWN

· ·

Blending the Three Ms

There are three fundamental elements that must be mixed together to make an ongoing profit-seeking enterprise. When they are blended in the proper proportions at the proper time, the business enterprise will succeed. When the mix is optimal, the business can blossom beyond human expectation. These elements are known as the three Ms.

1. *Money*—finances
2. *Men*—personnel
3. *Machines*—the function that produces your product or service.

Triangle of Small Business
MONEY

MEN   MACHINES

Marketing is the fourth M, but it is hidden within the 3M triangle. Marketing, or in other words, customers, is what holds the isosceles triangle together. The following rule describes the interrelationship among these three old truths.

• •

"The men who manage men manage the men who manage machines; but the men who manage money manage the men who manage men."

• •

In other words, these three elements are ranked in this order: (1) money, (2) men and (3) machines. It has been true since ancient times that money controls the people who control the machines.

Using Ratios To Create Leverage

Persuaders are great at keeping score. One of the ways they succeed is by watching the signals or predictors of future action. Everyone else watches raw numbers such as sales, profits, cash and debt, but persuaders watch ratios such as:

$$\frac{sales}{employee} \quad or \quad \frac{profit}{sales} \quad or \quad \frac{debt}{assets} \quad or \quad \frac{inventory}{turnover} \quad or \quad \frac{reward}{effort}$$

These ratios are important because they are early warning indicators. They watch balance. Persuaders obtain leverage by observing two variables at the same time as a ratio, and the net impact is much greater than just monitoring two isolated variables.

There are those who wonder what happened, those who watch what happens and those who make it happen. Rainmakers keep watch of ratios as they make things happen. Here is an example of how a rainmaker uses the profit/person ratio in the banking industry.

Profit/Person Ratio

Wilmington Trust was swamped and listing badly when Bernard J. Taylor II came on the board of the Delaware bank as CEO in 1979. More than half the assets were in long-term bonds, but high interest rates had sunk prices, leaving the liquidation value of the securities $609 million shy of the original purchase price. This was at a time when the bank had only $78 million in capital.

Bit by bit, Taylor sold off the bonds he could afford to unload and turned his attention to the other assets. As interest rates eased, for example, he refocused the bank on its profitable trust business and expanded into investment management. Using Wilmington's strong presence in the retail banking market as a base, he pushed hard into commercial lending by building up a staff that went out after business. (Is this shocking?)

At the same time, he streamlined the management structure. Once you would have needed to remove your shoes and socks to count all the levels between entry positions and the executive offices. Today, you can do it on one hand. To light a fire under his charges, the CEO established a liberal stock option incentive plan for executives and a discount stock purchase plan for everyone from teller to Taylor. Employees may put up 10 percent of their annual salary in Wilmington shares at a 15 percent discount to the market price.

Productivity blasted off. In 1980, each of the company's 1,936 employees generated $7,804 in profits. By 1986, the figure was $20,849, and in 1991 it reached $34,627. In Citicorp's best year on record (1988), it took 89,000 employees to earn $1.8 billion, an average of only $20,876 a head. The stock took off, too, from $3 a share in 1980 to $50.50 recently. By applying the profit/person ration Taylor was able to revive a failing institution.

4 *Negotiating Techniques*

"We are more than half of what we are by imitation. The great point is to choose good models and to study them with care."

LORD CHESTERFIELD

Herb Cohen—Master Negotiator

Another ancient principle of negotiation has been popularized by Herb Cohen of the Power Negotiation Institute in Skokie, Illinois. Herb is a stand-up comedian à la Henny Youngman, who delivers practical, straightforward negotiating advice. Herb's advice works because it's built around the laws of human behavior. He has appeared on TV and is the author of the bestselling book, *You Can Negotiate Anything*. His main negotiating advice is "to care, but not that much."

What Cohen means is that when you become obsessed with a negotiation, there is a lessened opportunity to arrive at a reasonable solution because you care so much that you can no longer be reasonable. That's why he likes to have third parties handle all negotiations. It's a good principle because it removes one level of emotion from the negotiation.

In fact, I arranged for him to speak to the CEO Clubs, and never once during the negotiations did Herb ever enter into the discussion. He had a third party handle his own negotiations. I like people who follow their own advice. He likes to emphasize this point with a story. He says, "When I'm paid to do a negotiation, I care, but not that much. I get paid no matter what the outcome." And he claims, "I am more effective because of it."

I think he's right. Entrepreneurial persuaders are always more effective in highly emotional negotiations by letting others deal directly with the other side. When heads of state meet, they do so to ratify what has already been negotiated. Never to negotiate but to celebrate a mutually agreeable deal.

Win-Win-Win Negotiations

Another favorite technique used by entrepreneurial persuaders is to negotiate a win-win settlement. This is a sound principle, but it's really better to work toward a win-win-*win* proposition. Negotiations that are concluded in this manner stay together.

Three levels of winning are necessary for a win-win-win negotiation: The universe as a whole has to win as well as both parties. Let's look at an example.

In the 1970s and 1980s, when the labor unions negotiated with the automotive manufacturers, both sides happily announced a new wage settlement every year without a strike. Everyone celebrated a win-win deal.

Unfortunately, during all those years of increased benefits and wages, productivity did not keep pace. While the unions and the automotive manufacturers were happy, wage increases were being passed on to consumers in the form of higher prices. The Japanese soon noticed that prices of U.S.-manufactured cars were too high. This left a gap that they were able to fill with lower wages and better manufacturing efficiency. So what may appear on the outside to be a win-win negotiation has to become a win-win-win negotiation to win in the long term.

Persuaders are more effective because they understand this need before the negotiating process begins, and they take it into account from the very beginning.

A Touch of Class

Real estate is the showcase of negotiations, and most folks would agree that over the long term, Trammel Crow of Dallas is one of the most successful real estate developers.

After any negotiation, but particularly after a long or bitter one, he waits one day; then he makes one more concession to his opponent. Obviously, this one wasn't coerced; it was given voluntarily after the agreement was reached.

It's a touch of class, and Trammel Crow is one of the best. He never considers this during the negotiation because he reasons it would cloud the deal and interfere with his ability to negotiate in top form. He cautions others not to think about this maneuver or to factor it into the negotiations as it could destroy your ability to conclude a deal. But it is usually possible to be generous after the deal is concluded.

Who Is Your Preferred Opponent?

I have asked many entrepreneurial negotiators whether they would rather negotiate against an experienced negotiator or an inexperienced one. You might think that they would choose a rookie opponent, but you'd be wrong. They unanimously prefer to deal with experienced negotiators.

Why?

First of all, an inexperienced negotiator may have to actually make good on all his or her bluffs. That is risky.

Second, a win-win-win settlement is more likely to occur if both sides are tuned to the same frequency right from the beginning. Oriental persuaders know this intuitively, but Americans learn it the hard way. The Oriental mind always takes longer to negotiate a settlement whereas the American mind wants to get it done in a ready-fire-aim mentality. Americans like to get close and then say, "Let's split the difference." The Japanese like to wait until everyone is fully satisfied. It's quite a difference. *When the rich person meets an experienced person in a negotiation, the experienced person gains a little money, and the rich person ends up with a little more experience.*

Leaders and Trailers

When you are negotiating, your language should reflect your willingness to listen, to give and take, and to consider alternatives. Good negotiators know how to frame their statements to achieve a win-win-win outcome.

One of the most effective ways to make a statement is to add a leader or trailer to it. These clauses cushion your statements by transforming them into questions, which are softer than pronouncements. Take a statement and sandwich it between both a leader and a trailer, and you have a persuasive statement that is actually a question.

Here are a few of each:

Leaders

"Would it be important to you . . . ?"
"Am I safe in assuming . . . ?"
"If there were a way . . . ?"
"Would you have an interest in . . . ?"
"Could you suggest . . . ?"
"Would you consider . . . ?"
"Have you ever tried . . . ?"
"Is it feasible to . . . ?"
"What would be . . . ?"
"Does it make sense to . . . ?"
"What you're really . . . ?"
"When do you think . . . ?"
"Is a more effective . . . ?"
"What would be the best way to . . . ?"

Trailers

"Is that correct?"
"Am I right?"
"Doesn't it?"
"Couldn't it?"
"Shouldn't it?"
"Wouldn't it?"
"Isn't it?"
"Does that make sense?"
"Fair enough?"
"Do you agree?"
"Is that important?"

"Is that accurate?"
"Is that on target?"
"Is that realistic?"
"Is that pertinent?"
"Is that relevant?"
"Is that clear?"
"Is that what you needed?"
"Would that be comfortable?"
"Do you understand?"

Negotiate for the Future

Another favorite ploy of entrepreneurial persuaders is to negotiate for something the other party can afford to give up. Never negotiate an unnegotiable demand. Always negotiate all the other demands where some small victory can be gained before you tackle the tough stuff. That way you'll make at least a little progress. This is a companion concept to the principle of the smallest possible inherent advantage (SPIA) outlined in Chapter 9.

When you negotiate, the secret is to make the pie bigger so that there can be more opportunities to exchange value. When you view the pie as a fixed size and argue only about the percentages being divided among the negotiators, you are already in a trap. A bigger pie gives many more opportunities and the ultimate opportunity to conclude with a win-win-win settlement.

A good technique for making the pie bigger (if you have exhausted all others) is to include the future. Sports teams have made the future a part of trades and thereby made famous the so-called "player-to-be-named later." This means, "We had a deal that wasn't quite right, so we threw in the adjusting player to be named later." Trading future draft choices is another example of using the future to conclude current negotiations.

Here is an example a little closer to home. Let's say that your college alma mater calls to ask you to volunteer to return to the school for a week to head a telemarketing fundraising campaign for alumni. If they ask you to do it in two or three weeks, you will probably refuse. But if they ask you to do it nine months from now, on a Tuesday, and offer to pay the expenses you are more likely to agree. *It shows that you are more willing to accept something for the future than you are right now.* That's a very important negotiating principle that all persuaders know intuitively.

Here's how I put it to work just a few months ago.

I rent a penthouse for my business in Manhattan. It's in a spectacular setting with panoramic views of Manhattan and a 4,000-square-foot outdoor terrace with trees and a swimming pool. It is the headquarters for my two associations, The Center for Entrepreneurial Management (CEM) and the Chief Executive Officers Clubs (CEOs). I like to say that I have no desire to leave because I'm on top of the world. Members come from all over the world to party at the penthouse.

However, being on the seventeenth floor with only one elevator accessible to this penthouse has some disadvantages. There was a major elevator renovation in the building a few months ago and I was deprived of an elevator for more than half a year. It created a serious disruption in service and was a violation of the lease agreement. However, when the new elevator was eventually installed, it improved the service to this floor considerably. The landlord and I had a long negotiation over the fact that my service was disrupted during this long period of repair. We couldn't agree on a reduction in rent that made both parties happy. Neither wanted to go to court and leave the settlement in the hands of an unknowing party.

The compromise solution acceptable to both of us was to extend CEM's lease on the space from ten years to eleven. It was a win-win-win negotiation.

The logic is beautiful. There was a one-year disruption of service during the ten-year lease. Rather than try to find an economic justification for just how much that is worth, or going to court to fight to see who wins, CEM and the landlord agreed to extend the lease. That way CEM had ten good years and one bad year. The period when the elevators were under repair was swapped for a good year in the eleventh year. This is an example of using the future to solve an existing negotiation. Winning now is factored against winning later.

Mirroring—I Like You

We are most comfortable with the familiar. We like people to look like us, act like us and talk like us. When strangers talk with an accent, it's not uncommon to say they talk "funny." The reason we call people we haven't met *strangers* is that they look strange to us.

One of the most effective techniques of a persuader is mirroring. What it says, in essence, is that we like people who behave as we do. And when we like someone, we are more prone to do what that person wants to do.

The great hypnotherapist, Dr. Milton Erickson, learned to mirror the breathing patterns, posture, tonality and gestures of other people. By doing that, he achieved a totally binding rapport in a matter of minutes. People who did not know him suddenly trusted him without question.

So how do you mirror another person? What kinds of physical traits can you mirror? Start with the voice. Mirror his tonality, phrasing, pitch and volume. Pick up on how fast he talks, what sort of pauses he makes and favorite words or phrases. Mirror posture, breathing patterns, eye contact, body language, facial expressions, hand gestures or other distinctive movements. Any aspect of physiology, from the way a person plants his feet to the way he tilts his head, can be mirrored.

You don't have to mirror everything about a person to create rapport. You can start with the tone of voice or a facial expression.

When you watch an entrepreneur persuading another person, observe how often he or she mirrors the person in a natural way. When the person removes his glasses, the entrepreneur removes or touches his glasses. When the other person scratches, the entrepreneur scratches. Mirroring is a natural act of an entrepreneurial persuader.

Why do parents of newborn babies claim their baby looks like them? It always brings a smile. In fact, newborn babies all look alike. Much more alike than they look like one of their parents. Just take a photograph of a newborn baby at a hospital and then see if anyone can match it to the proper parents, and you'll see.

Nonverbal Communication

Although 93 percent of all communication is nonverbal, 93 percent of preparation time is usually spent on the verbal portion of communication. It's opposite to the logic. When you want something to happen, your whole being has to want it. The words you say are never as important as the way you say them. Remember that you can say, *I* love you, I *love* you, or I love *you*.

Understanding nonverbal communications and being sensitive to signals radiating from the other communicator are key skills of an effective persuader. When your arms are folded and legs crossed, it usually means that your mind is closed. When your arms and hands are wide open, your heart and mind are probably open too.

An excellent book on this subject is Gerard Nierenberg's *Metatalk: How To Uncover the Hidden Meaning in What People Say*, published by the Negotiation Institute (341 Madison, New York, NY 10017, 212/986-5555). It's a handbook with visual detail and pictures of the various methods of nonverbal communication. The author discusses not just gestures but clusters of gestures.

The Most Powerful Three-Letter Word in This Book

• •

"The important thing is not to stop questioning. Curiosity has its own reason for existing."

ALBERT EINSTEIN

• •

What if there were a three-letter word that guaranteed:

- the key to winning the law of averages
- advice from mentors
- perceived equality from professionals
- increased marketing results
- better marital and family relations

- increased wealth
- positive publicity
- savings on purchases
- power of a persuader with a purpose

You would probably want to know it, wouldn't you? The word is *ask*: Ask and it shall be given. Seek and you shall find. Knock and the door shall be opened.

Young children understand the importance of this word. The average child asks sixty questions a day. The average college graduate, on the other hand, asks two questions a day, and one of them is "Where is the bathroom?"

If You Want To Sell, Ask, Don't Tell

Inc. magazine named Steven Jobs, the founder of Apple Computer and NEXT, Entrepreneur of the Decade. They also named Mitchell Kapor, founder of Lotus Development and the new president of On Technology, Best Entrepreneur in the Software Business. I disagree.

My vote for both would go to Bill Gates of Microsoft. My reasoning is based upon a quote from Brad Silverberg, Microsoft's vice president in charge of the Windows development program. He said: "Bill Gates has the laser-like ability to home in on the absolute right question to ask. He'll know some intricate lower-level detail about a program and makes you wonder, 'How does he know that—some piece of code or piece of technology Microsoft is not even involved in?' "

Entrepreneurial persuaders do more and accomplish more because they are superstars at asking the right questions at the right time. *This is the key to persuasion, and you can never do it often enough or well enough. If you don't ask, the answer is no.*

Questioning Techniques

Most people agree that questioning is at the heart of the persuasive process, but few people can tell you how to ask better questions.

My vote for best "asker" on television goes to the rumpled, raincoated Lieutenant Columbo, played by Peter Falk. Watching this series is the best way I know to improve your questioning skills.

If it is still being shown in your area, tune in and write down the questions Columbo asks. Number them sequentially, and add an asterisk to the last question he always asks in a sequence. That's the one where he holds one of his arms in the air and says, "Oh, I almost forgot." This last-minute gesture diminishes the importance of this question. It's the key question, but he makes it look like an afterthought. When you analyze only Columbo's questions, you'll see question sequences, question clusters and the same questions asked a dozen ways to see if the answers could be different. This is how the little Italian genius finally solves the mystery. He is the best "asker" on T.V.

Entrepreneurial persuaders have better hearing, and in combination with better questioning they simply get better results.

Asking the Right Question Is Only Half the Battle

Asking the right questions in the right sequence is only half the battle. The second most important word in this book, and in life, is *listen*. Failure at either causes failure in communication.

A good example of listening but not hearing occurred during the negotiations that eventually ended the Vietnam war. Right from the start you could tell what was going to happen because both sides had different attitudes about each other's position. The Americans checked into a posh Paris hotel and set themselves up for a short negotiation. There weren't many issues as far as they were concerned. Meantime, the Vietnamese came with only a few people, and the first thing they did was to buy a villa just outside Paris. The two sides couldn't even agree on the shape of the negotiating table. How long do you think the negotiations lasted?

The words that are spoken in a negotiation are seldom as important as the actions that are taken. You must hear from these actions as well as from the words. The joint announcements issued during a negotiation seldom predict its success. Rather, the real signs of success come from the manner in which the information is presented. Do the protagonists speak together? Who speaks first? Do they issue one common or two separate announcements? These are the real signs of progress, and they must be heard along with the words.

The Secret To Raising Capital for Entrepreneurial Persuaders

Here's the situation: You've been in a financial negotiation for three months, but the deal just won't close. You've got a terrific business plan—even your venture capitalist admits that—but no matter what you do, you just can't come to terms. Half of you is thinking, "Maybe I should just get up from the table and leave the room." But the other half of you is thinking, "I've got three months invested in this deal, they've got the money, they like my plan. I'd be a fool not to stick it out." What do you do? Well, there's a seven-word phrase that will help you close the deal. But before I tell you what it is, I need to show you how and why it works.

The biggest mistake an entrepreneur can make in dealing with a venture capitalist is to lose sight of what every financial source is really after. It may sound like the person wants too much equity or too much control, but what it really comes down to is money—his job and his goal is to make a profit on his investments. So when the venture capitalist makes what you consider an unreasonable offer, don't panic. You don't have to give up control of your business in order to get financed.

But what *do* you try next? Do you shop the deal around, hoping to arouse enough interest to play one source off against the other? That might be a good ploy in theory, but in reality it tends to alienate venture capitalists rather than entice them.

Then what's the secret to closing the deal? Good old-fashioned persistence? I have always subscribed to the theory that if a batter stands in the batter's box long enough, some dumb pitcher will eventually hit the bat with the ball. But all by itself, *persistence won't raise a nickel. It must be combined with persuasion.*

Maybe you should get the financier to restate everything that looks good about the deal and attracted him or her to it in the first place. That will bring you back to square one, but it won't get you any closer to closing the deal than you were when you started. That's because as special as you may think your deal is, chances are that the venture capitalist has seen, and maybe even turned down, similar deals in the past.

Getting your business off the ground might be your dream, but the art of raising capital doesn't involve selling dreams. It involves reducing risk!

When their backs are against the wall during negotiations, dream sellers say something like, "You ought to see how beautiful this summer home is. It fronts on the lake and has a . . ." But that's not the way raising capital works. In fact, it's just the opposite. When you're back is to the wall, you want to be able to say, "The risk on this deal is zero—the downside is zero. Now let's talk about the upside."

I recall a negotiation over a small equity investment in a retail liquor store. When the negotiation reached the eleventh hour and was at the go–no-go decision, the liquor store owner closed the deal with classic risk-reducing humor. He said, "Hell, you could always drink your way out of the investment if it went bad!"

The following four examples illustrate techniques for raising capital.

Land Sales

I have a 100-acre piece of ocean-front property in Nova Scotia. I bought the land 18 months ago for $100,000, but now I need cash, so I decided to sell off half of it. I divided it into two parcels of equal value and put one of the parcels on the market. What do you think the asking price was?

If you guessed $100,000, you guessed right. And what this illustrates is perhaps the single most important thing to remember about persuading investors. An investor's first and foremost concern in making an investment lies in getting his or her money back. Investors aren't just in the business of making investments. They're also in the business of recouping their investments. It's the way you can tell the good ones apart from the losers.

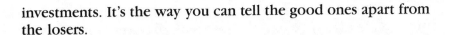

> *"The only treaties that ought to count are those which would effect a settlement between ulterior motives."*
>
> PAUL VALÉRY, GREATNESS AND THE DECADENCE OF EUROPE, 1931

Gambling

Here's a second example: Did you ever watch the gamblers in the Las Vegas or Atlantic City casinos? Most of them are sensible enough people when they're at home, but put them at a slot machine or a crap table and they go crazy. If you watch long enough, you'll notice that a funny thing begins to happen with some of them. At about two or three o'clock in the morning, they pull all the money out of their pockets, put it down on a table and count it. They divide it into two piles and put one of the piles back into their pocket. Then they continue to play with the other pile of money. What did they put back into their pocket? Cab fare? Money to call home? No. What all smart gamblers put back into their pocket is their initial stake—the money they came with. Remember that a fool and his or her money are soon parted.

Venture Capitalist

In my third example I'll show you how the best money raisers in the world raise money. These are the venture capitalists. A successful venture capitalist can pick up the phone and raise $100 million in less than an hour. Most entrepreneurs have trouble getting someone to co-sign a $10,000 note.

I speak at a number of conferences where venture capitalists assemble, and it's always interesting to watch two of the giants come into the room. When they do meet, what do you think they say? Let's say that Arthur Rock (West Coast) runs into Fred Adler (East Coast). What do you think they talk about? Does Fred say that he made $600 million in the last quarter? Does Arthur say that his average annual rate of return for the past 17 years has been 41.26 percent? No. What they talk about is the success of their *last* fund.

Fred Adler may run several funds of $100 million to $200 million each, but Arthur Rock is interested only in Fred's most current fund. The rest is history. So Fred might say, "I understand you put together $200 million for Fund 6." And Arthur will say, "Yes, that's true." Then Fred will ask, "Well, how long did it take you to get the principal back to your partners in that fund?" Arthur might answer, "Eleven months." Then Arthur will ask Fred how long it took his last fund to get its principal back to his partners. And so on and so on. The only thing that venture capitalists ever compare is how fast they returned the original investment back to their partners.

When the gambler puts his original capital back into his pocket, he's doing the same thing as the venture capitalist. He returns the original investment and continues playing on his winnings. Of course, the venture capitalists are a little more sophisticated. They raise their money in ten-year limited partnerships, but their strategy is the same. They try to rush the original investment back to their partners as soon as possible, and then they play with the winnings for the balance of the ten-year period. The partners usually have to wait the full ten years to get their winnings, but they get their principal back right away.

Initial Public Offering (IPO)

Now let me offer one last example. Let's say a young company goes public at $10 a share, but a few months after the initial public offering (IPO) the company runs into some problems and the stock drops to $5 a share. The entrepreneur works hard to get the earnings and the stock price back up. Eventually, the earnings reach, and even begin to exceed, the original projections. But after a slow climb back up, the stock price hits $10 and then just sits there. It is stuck at that price because, despite the company's strong performance, the stockholders (investors) remember the initial setback, and when the stock returns to its original price, they begin to bail out. It is known as the "jump-off" point—the point at which they can recoup their initial investment. In this case, the entrepreneur isn't left with any winnings to play with, but at least he has recovered his initial investment and is ready to start over again.

Despite the very different approaches of these four categories of investors—the landowner, gambler, venture capitalist and investors in IPO stocks—their thinking is the same: Protect the original capital. They all want to make sure the risk on their investment is held to a minimum.

So, after you've tried everything you know to close a deal and it still seems to be at an impasse, try my seven-word phrase and see what happens. Tell him, *"You will get your money back first, and then . . ."*

Negotiating for Control

A negative trait inherent in all rainmakers is the need to be in control. They view life as an ongoing series of small and large negotiations. They seldom take the time to smell the roses.

For the past dozen years, Chester L. Karrass of California and his son, Gary, have run a successful business giving thousands of seminars on the art of negotiation. The headline on their advertisement reads: "In Business You Don't Get What You Deserve, You Get What You Negotiate." One of their central messages, and the subject of Chester's doctoral dissertation, which launched this business, is setting the opening condition. In a simple example, if you are selling your home, there is a delicate trade-off of beginning the selling process with too high a price, which could scare off potential buyers, and setting a price that allows room to give in to close the sale. Karrass maintains that 90 percent of the sellers do not start with a high enough asking price to allow a successful negotiation to result in the sale of the house.

According to real estate professionals, here is how most people set the asking price for their home:

Too High	Just Right	Too Low	Total
15%	50%	35%	100%

Notice that the tendency to begin too low outweighs the tendency to set too high by more than two to one. This shows again why entrepreneurial persuaders succeed where others fail.

Entrepreneurial persuaders set it too high about 90 percent of the time. They do it not only because they are optimistic, which they are; it's more an issue of control: They set it too high to stay in control. When you set it too high, you think you are in control, but when it is set too low, you think you have little control.

It's like drafting a legal document after a prolonged negotiation. The question is, should you or the other party draw up the agreement? It costs a little more to have your lawyer do it, but it's an issue of control. Given a choice, an entrepreneurial persuader will always choose to have his or her legal team draw up the legal papers. This is such a central issue that the legal system tries to "even the score" by establishing the following precedent: "If a legal issue is vague in the Agreement, it will be ruled against the party that initially drew it up."

That tells you how important this issue of control is in practice.

• •

"Treaties are observed as long as they are in harmony with interests."

NAPOLEON I, MAXIMS

• •

A related negotiating principle is less uniformly applicable. It states that in any negotiation, the first party that mentions price loses. This ties in with the preceding argument about control because it is also about establishing the initial condition. It's the asking price question from another angle.

This principle works with product advertising as well. Which of these two products would you like to buy? They offer identical benefits:

Product 1—$99

Product 2—~~$139~~ Now $99!

Did you ever watch a Tony Robbins infomercial? When the part comes to selling the books and tapes, it usually starts out with the words "Although you'd expect a product like this to cost over $500, we have reduced the price to. . ." Persuaders know that value is a perceived concept.

A Management Course for CEOs

The CEO Clubs sponsor a three-day management course that contrasts two management styles—entrepreneurial versus professional—in a debate format.

One of the faculty, Ronald Myers, extols the virtues of professional management. He also prepares the course notebook and drafts the agenda. Every year he cheats a little to get more time on the podium.

By volunteering to draft the agenda, he steals a little control from the opposing speaker. He always errs by giving himself too much time, and it's my job every year, as the host, to cut back his requests.

It's like setting budgets or the asking price to sell a home. You can never ask for enough in a budget because it just has to be reduced. It's all a matter of control, and nobody sets it higher or does it better than an entrepreneurial persuader.

• •

"The persuasion of a friend is a strong thing."

HOMER, ILIAD, *9TH CENTURY B.C.*

• •

Ron's Rules for Meetings

Ron Myers has developed an excellent set of rules to control a meeting. The rainmaker needs to be in control not only in one-on-one or selling situations but in meetings as well. Although you might think that rules limit control, they actually increase control and freedom when they are universally observed. Following are Ron Myers' rules for meetings:

1. *Agree on objectives.* What do we want to have accomplished by the time we walk out of here?
2. *Establish a time frame. . .* and then let's try to cut it in half. Where meetings are concerned, haste isn't always waste.
3. *Stick to the subject.* Where is this discussion going? What decision are we trying to make?
4. *New input only.* We probably don't need to hear your views several times in order to appreciate their importance.
5. *Bottom line first.* We want your conclusions; we may not need to hear all the reasoning behind them.
6. *One conversation at a time.* We can't afford distractions, and it's unfair to the person whose attention you're borrowing.
7. *No snide remarks.* Someone's feelings could get hurt for no good reason.
8. *Silence is consent.* Speak now, or forever hold your peace.

My Favorite Negotiating Lessons

There are several things you should never observe in their formative stages because no matter how good they eventually turn out, the process of making them can be repulsive.

1. sausage
2. laws
3. negotiating lessons
4. books

This is a true story of the sale of a little company in Sturbridge, Massachusetts, to a big company in Palo Alto, California. Although it happened in 1979, all the key players are still in place in 1992.

Coherent, Inc., headed by Jim Hobart, chairman, and Hank Gauthier, president, bought a little company called Laser, Inc., headed by Al Battista and Bill Shiner. I was a founder, small shareholder and director of Laser, Inc., but I was an adviser, not a player.

One day, the major shareholder, Al Battista, announced he wanted out; he was tired of the problems of being a small company's president. It immediately became my job to sell it.

We had a book value of less than $100,000, and during five years in business we had not made much money. Our sales were under $1 million, but we believed we had good technology and a rosy future.

There were only a handful of potential buyers, and I contacted each of them via a form letter. Here is what the letter said:

> We have been approached to sell our business, and that's what prompted this letter. While the opportunity presented to us is not perfect, it is acceptable and we are beginning the process to consummate an arrangement.
>
> We are very familiar with (insert name of company) and your people and your product line. It occurs to us that you and your business would be a better strategic fit for us. However, we do not know if you or your business are interested.
>
> I am handling this situation for the two principals, for I am also a director for the business. Please contact me immediately if you are interested as the process of transferring ownership is already underway.
>
> Please keep this information confidential.

Note that the letter does not tell all the truth all the time. (Refer to my comments about the "con" aspect of entrepreneurial persuasion in Chapter 1.)

Coherent responded to the letter and arranged for its two principals (Hank and Jim) to visit the company on the evening of an East Coast trip. They spent about six hours in Sturbridge, and during this time they decided to buy the business. Remember what I said earlier: The first one to mention price loses. So price was not discussed at this meeting. Not once. They didn't even drop their guard and ask me in the privacy of the two-hour car ride back to Boston's Logan Airport.

A few weeks later, Al Battista and I were invited to Palo Alto, California, to negotiate the sale of the business. On the plane, we locked on to a simple strategy we called "the big bluff." Here's how it worked:

1. We would say that we have an offer now on the table of $1 million.
2. We would say that we'd rather sell to Coherent because we like the people, the products and the company better. Actually, this was true.
3. We would never tell who made this fictitious offer of $1 million.
4. We would say that we were going to sell the company, very soon, possibly in the next month.
5. Al and I both had to agree to a deal even though Al had majority control. The other major shareholder, Bill Shiner, did not come to the session as someone had to run the business.

It was our job to sell the company for $1 million. Our justification for not telling all the truth all the time was that we wanted to get the highest price possible for the company. In hindsight, we might have secured the same objectives using different means, but I don't think we would have sold at a cheaper price.

The West Coast meeting began in the Coherent conference room. The star of the show was their corporate counsel and a Coherent director, attorney Larry Sonsini.

Most of the six-hour day was spent with Sonsini at the blackboard doing various financial calculations, showing a fair market value of Laser, Inc. He used book value, market value, and liquidation value and even a generous Sonsini value! No matter how hard he tried, he just couldn't get the value of the business much above $200,000. And this was five times below our asking price of $1 million. After all, he was working with a balance sheet that had about $100,000 of book value. His numbers were accurate and his approach was fair. He was right and we were wrong.

As the day ended, and we had a return flight to catch, we all concluded that there would be no deal, as a 500 percent price difference meant we were not only not in the same ballpark— we were not even in the same league. We all threw up our hands in disappointment and frustration.

As we were boarding the cab, the real decision makers, Hank and Jim, came out and asked us to stay a little longer. "We'll meet your current offer," they said.

They bought Laser, Inc., for $1 million in 1979, and they overpaid for it significantly. However, one year after the purchase, they both told me that it was one of their best long-term investments ever. The company blossomed, and Coherent recouped its investment 1,000 times over. So in the final analysis, it was cheap.

Again, in 1992, all four principals are still working for Coherent, and Laser, Inc., is now called Coherent General in Sturbridge, Massachusetts.

The following statements were made during the negotiations. Each one is a negotiating jewel.

1. Gosh, Mr. Sonsini, that analysis was brilliant, but Mr. Jack Klouts, our neighbor across the street, sold his company for $1 million, and it certainly wasn't as good as mine.
2. I don't know why I want $1 million, but I guess there is something magic about big, round numbers.
3. Is it permissible for Joe and me to be here in the room without a lawyer while you have an attorney present? We don't want to do anything illegal that could overturn the agreement.
4. I didn't know that you were going to bring a bad guy (Attorney Sonsini). Our attorney, Dennis O'Connor, is still in Boston. Should we ask him to come out to talk with Mr. Sonsini?
5. I don't really know who suggested the $1 million price originally, but that's the offer on the table.
6. Doesn't it happen that most small companies valued around $1 million actually get sold for $1 million? You

know, if it's worth, let's say, $500,000 to $1.5 million, the actual price gravitates towards a million?

7. I don't really want to negotiate too hard with you now because I'll have to work for you later, and I don't want you to think less of me because of this negotiation. I'm trying hard to be reasonable.

8. This is not a lot of money to you, but to us it means whether or not we can afford to do business with you. It's life and death to us.

9. I'm sorry, but we can't really tell you much about the other offer just as we can't tell *them* much about you! Do you understand?

10. To tell you the truth, we'd really like to sell to you because we like you and your company better. If it were a $10 million sales price, we could afford that luxury. But given the price of only $1 million, we are on the edge of being financially responsible to our families.

All of these comments blend logic and emotion in an unusual balance. All of them can help you to persuade better, but you must accept the harsh reality that entrepreneurial persuasion, as opposed to other types, incorporate some of the "con." Persuasion requires the other party to see things not as they are but as what you want them to be. As Professor Karl Vespar, the faculty superstar at the University of Washington in Seattle, says, the difference between entrepreneurs and cons lies in the degree of long-term value.

• •

"If the horn cannot be twisted, the ear can."

MALAY PROVERB

• •

An Agent with Limited Authority

One of the most popular negotiating ploys employed by all persuaders is to send an agent with limited authority. Attorney Larry Sonsini was an example of such an agent, disguised as a director and adviser to Coherent, which tended to cloud his actual level of authority. Technically, you can't lose a negotiation when you send an agent with limited authority. After all, limited authority means the agent can't finalize a deal. The best cure for negotiating with such an agent is to ask questions. These questions will help later when the decision makers arrive.

Attorney Gerard Nierenberg, the founder of the Negotiation Institution in New York City (along with his partner, Richard Zief), suggests handling an agent with limited authority as follows. Again, it involves not telling all the truth all the time.

He is going to Los Angeles from New York, but he must give a three-hour seminar in Chicago on his way to the West Coast. He wants to bring a box of books with him to Los Angeles without the stop in Chicago. When he explains this to the gate agent at the airport, the agent with limited authority says, "Sorry, the baggage must travel with the passenger." Then Nierenberg explains his desire to have the box of books go directly to Los Angeles while he stops off for a few hours in Chicago. The agent again says, "It's against the rules, sorry." Dealing with agents with limited authority can be frustrating. They are immune to the music from the pied piper's flute.

Nierenberg shows how to handle the same agent by using his broad range of baffle. He approaches the agent with a question: "Suppose *you* were going to Los Angeles and had to stop off in Chicago for a few hours, but you wanted your luggage to go directly to Los Angeles. How would you do that?"

"Easy," responds the gate agent. "Just come up to me and say 'I'm in a hurry and I'm going to Los Angeles. Will you get this luggage to the flight real quick so I don't miss it?' Then you can give me your ticket and get a boarding pass after the luggage is gone."

5 Motivating To Make Things Happen

"Birds of a feather flock together."

ARISTOTLE

Picture a pied piper playing a flute, marching the high step along a winding country road. Following the leader is a long string of successful people marching in single file, happy and smiling. Everybody's happy and life is good.

Create the same scene in your mind again, but this time, intersperse various animals in what has become a rag-tag marching line of followers. Monkeys, donkeys, turkeys and skunks scattered among the long line of happy followers spoil the picture. It becomes not a line of winners following a playful pied piper but a disjointed group of outcasts from an animal farm.

Get Rid of the Turkeys

Leaders are judged by the quality of their followers. Rainmakers associate with chiefs, heads of hunting parties and other rainmakers. It is impossible to soar with the eagles when your day-to-day existence is filled with turkeys.

You have to take concrete action to get rid of turkeys. They won't disappear all by themselves. Yet too many people choose to do nothing when a turkey comes into their lives.* They find it offensive to their nature to be offensive. People with a purpose, especially those with the power of persuasion, refuse to accept that living with turkeys is a necessary part of their existence. So let the turkeys play gobble-gobble with other turkeys. You stay with the eagles.

Once you know you are among the eagles, be the kind of person who causes people to like themselves more when they are with you. It's really an extension of the Golden Rule: "Do unto others as you would have others do unto you." Entrepreneurial persuaders make things happen by inspiring those around them to feel at their peak performance.

Get Rid of the Monkeys

It's not always what entrepreneurial persuaders do that makes a difference. It's also what they don't do. They are experts at not accepting monkeys. Too many of us accumulate so many monkeys hanging on our backs that we just can't seem to maneuver comfortably. Dragging them around slows us down. And there are more monkeys around every corner. Entrepreneurial persuaders don't accept monkeys, even when they are offered as gifts.

Here's an example: A coworker is excited about a trip she just took. She brought back a business plan about a new company and a new situation. It's 140 pages, quite detailed, and the coworker tries to get you excited as well. She says, "I'm going to give you this whole plan to read. Let's talk about it when we get together next week."

Don't take that monkey. It will slow you to a crawl. Rather, say, "I'm willing to take the whole document if you will also give me a one-page outline of what's in it, what's substantive about it, what you want me to look for, what to do about it and

---

*One of history's greatest rainmakers made only one mistake in his life. But fortunately this error in judgment was overshadowed by his accomplishments. Benjamin Franklin lobbied to have the turkey established as the national bird. Thank goodness he lost out to the eagle.

what pages you think are key. And if you'd use a yellow marker to note the highlights, I'll be sure not to miss them."

This strategy focuses your time by taking the heavy-duty work away from you and shifting it to your coworker's initiation. It reduces your job from five hours to fifteen minutes. This avoidance must be a 24-hour-a-day, seven-day-a-week alert.

Entrepreneurial persuaders strive to delegate work to other people. They don't take on more work just because it may have a higher profit margin. They know the ideal business is one in which everyone else does the work, and they just count the money.

A direct mail operation using infomercials on television is a wonderful example. Once the ad is made, most of these entrepreneurial persuaders have someone to schedule the ads, someone else to take the telephone calls, another source to ship the products and even someone to deposit the funds automatically into their bank accounts. Their goal is to do *only* the essential job, which is to produce the half-hour ads. That's the heart and brains of the business. They do that and let others do what they do best.

Joe Sugarman

Joe Sugarman is the legendary direct mail wizard behind the Northbrook, Illinois, company known as JS&A. Joe has been a speaker for the CEO Clubs and is currently the facilitator of the Chicago CEO Club's presidential advisory council. His current business is selling Blu Blocker sunglasses, which he advertises on his half-hour TV infomercials. His message is so captivating that I bought two pairs at $50 each.

Joe knows what it takes to manage a highly successful company and continue to make it work. He employs fewer than 15 people. Joe's job is to do the infomercials, and he hires others to do everything else. He doesn't like turkeys or monkeys and knows how to delegate the work.

Rainmakers make rain for the animals, and that's their only association with them. You'll find the rainmakers smoking peace pipes at the powwows. That's their natural habitat.

Motivating by Speaking

• •

"The ancestor of every action is a thought."

RALPH WALDO EMERSON

• •

What's the best speech you ever heard? Who was the greatest motivator of all time? Although his message was truly barbaric, Adolph Hitler was a truly powerful motivational speaker—maybe the most powerful of all time. He understood the connection between speech and action.

In my seminars, I ask participants to identify the most important part of a motivational speech. Is it the beginning, middle or close?

About a third of the participants say the introduction, a third say the middle and a third say the close. So you can see there is no popular consensus that one of the three segments is more important than the other two. Politicians (who don't like to take a position) say that all three segments are equally important. And for once they are right.

All three components of a speech are important because a speech is more than the sum of its parts. It's not like a triathalon in which you combine the score of each competition to determine an overall score. It's an event in and of itself. Hence, you cannot break it down and treat it as three separate parts.

The most important part of a motivational speech is actually a *fourth* component: *what the audience does after the speech*.

Some 2,500 years ago, the Greek orator Demosthenes said that a speech has only three purposes: action, action and action. This Athenian said it first, and Adolph Hitler did it best. They persuaded people by giving speeches.

There were two great orators of ancient times, Demosthenes and Cicero. The audiences always cheered Cicero's speeches, but when Demosthenes concluded, the crowds said: "Let us march!" and they did. That's the difference between a presentation and a persuasion.

These days, most information can be transmitted more effectively in written form or electronically. But when you want people to take action, it is better to use a speech. A person's presence can cause action much more quickly and effectively than a letter or tape. Persuaders know this instinctively.

Persuaders are legendary for being able to create action from a speech. It's one of their finest skills. If you have ever heard Zig Ziglar, a popular motivational speaker who often gets his audience to jump up and down, you'd realize that he couldn't have the same impact if he wrote his talk out ahead of time and handed it to you to read. The *way* the message is communicated makes it valuable. The objective is to create action by using more than the content of the words.

For more information on public speaking, I recommend three sources:

1. Past CEO Club speaker Brent Filson's book, *Executive Speeches—How 51 CEOs Did Theirs*. Contact him at: 505 White Oaks Rd., Williamstown, MA 01267-2223, 413/458-5285.
2. National Speakers Association (NSA), 4747 N. Seventh St., Phoenix, AZ 85014 602/265-1001.
3. Dottie Walters' newsletter, *Sharing Ideas* (Royal Publishing, Box 1120, Glendora, CA 91740, 818/335-8069).

Motivation Theories

• •

"A musician must make music, an artist must paint, a poet must write, if he is to be ultimately at peace with himself."

ABRAHAM MASLOW

• •

In the sixth century B.C., the Greeks were already teaching motivation. Aesop set the stage with a fable contrasting the north wind and the sun's different motivational styles. To settle who was stronger they proposed a contest. Their objective was to motivate a man traveling along the road below to remove his cloak. The wind's approach was to blow the cloak off. But the harder the wind blew, the tighter the man held the cloak about him. He blew until the man stood dead in his tracks and the wind grew tired. The wind concluded the man was beyond motivation and quit. The sun smiled and took his turn, beaming warmth and encouragement for the man on his travels. The man's rate of progress increased, and soon he removed his cloak to better enjoy the sun's attention. Aesop's moral? For results, satisfy a person's basic needs, assume he or she wants to succeed, share a common objective, show high concern for the individual as well as the objective and make the task satisfying.

Five landmark motivational philosophies have refined Aesop's simple observation.

1. Abraham Maslow explained that everyone has a hierarchy of needs. You cannot motivate people to achieve greatness until you've met their basic needs.
2. In 1953, Douglas McGregor wrote about Theory X and Theory Y. X assumes employees don't want to work and have to be coerced; Y assumes employees want to work and will work better if they have a say in how they meet their objectives.
3. In 1954, Peter Drucker saw management by objectives as the only principle that would give full scope to individual strength and responsibility. Myriad MBO/MBA management mavens sprang forth to help organizations establish systems of measurable, mutually agreed-upon goals.
4. 1964 gave us Blake and Mouton's Management Grid expressing motivation in terms of a manager's concern for people or production. The best management shows high concern for both.
5. In 1966, Frederick Herzberg's Motivation-Hygiene theory struck at the prevailing philosophies. Focus on job enrichment and emphasize things that lead to employee achievement, recognition, satisfaction, responsibility, advancement and growth rather than fixing on the hygiene matters of company policy, supervision, work conditions and salary.

Following is a brief summary of each philosophy.

Maslow's Hierarchy of Needs

The psychologist Abraham Maslow recognized humans as a wanting animal. As soon as one need is satisfied we seek to fill yet a higher need. Our needs are organized in a series of levels like a pyramid (see figure 5.1). At the base are physiological needs—the need to survive. When motivated by thirst, hunger or the need for shelter, we have no interest in anything else. Satisfy these needs, and "safety" needs such as eliminating danger, threat and insecurity become the primary motivation. Satisfy these, and we become motivated by the social needs of group membership, acceptance by others and mutual love. Egoistic needs—a need for status and importance—are very strong motivators but only after the lower needs on the pyramid are met. Maslow's highest level of need is self-actualization. Here, at last, is the motivation to be creative and fulfill our potential—to contribute something worthwhile.

The motivational challenge is to create a work environment providing all the Maslow needs: a living wage, job security, team environment, recognition and self-fulfillment. You cannot skip a need. Enable every employee from entry clerk to chief executive to work toward self-actualization, and the resultant organization fulfillment will be beyond the dreams of avarice.

McGregor's Theory X and Theory Y

Douglas McGregor says most management thinking is mistakenly based on the concept that people do not want to work and leaders can get work from them only by reward or punishment. He called this Theory X.

Theory X employees are gullible, indifferent, resistant to change, self-centered and lazy. The carrot-and-stick approach is the only way to motivate them. Theory X works best in the military in time of war.

Theory Y maintains that people are *not* by nature passive or resistant to organizational needs. They have become so only because of their business world experience. All people have within them the motivation, the potential for development, the

Figure 5.1   Maslow's Hierarchy of Needs

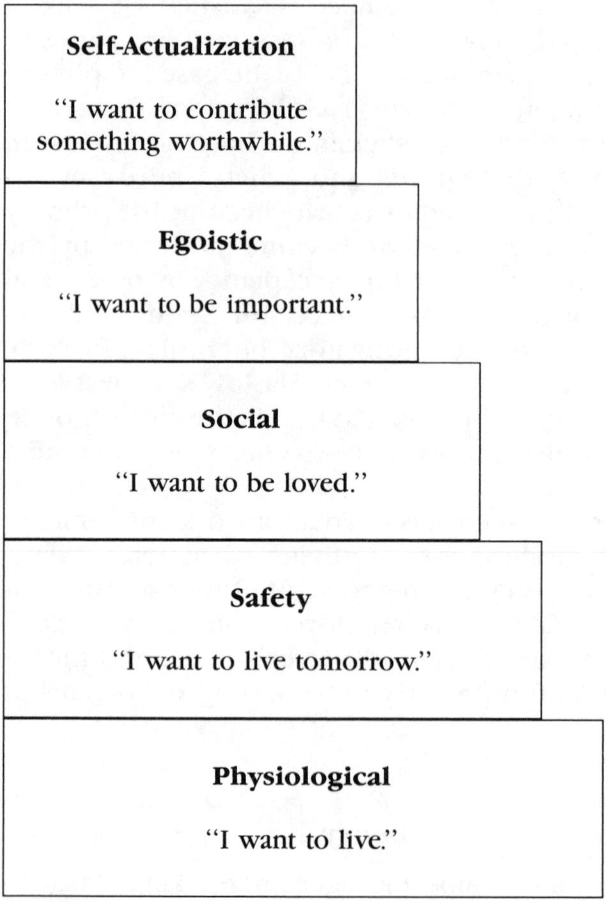

capacity for assuming responsibility and the ability and willingness to direct their behavior toward organizational goals. McGregor believes that people will work because they want to work. He feels that if workers have a chance to decide their own methods and are allowed to use their full capacities, management will get the best results. Theory Y has been popular in managing academic institutions.

Drucker's Management by Objectives (MBO)

In his breakthrough book, *The Practice of Management*, Peter Drucker suggests: "What the business enterprise needs is a principle of management that will give full scope to individual strength and responsibility, and at the same time give common direction of vision and effort, establish team work and harmonize the goals of the individual with the common weal [benefit]."

MBO and self-control are the only principles that can do this. Employees develop their own objectives and participate in setting their organization's objectives as well. This ensures that their personal objectives harmonize with the company's. For the same reason employees must understand the objectives of their business unit. Challenging, achievable and relevant objectives get defined at every level of the organization.

Employees achieve self-control through measurement. Each objective has a set of quantifiable measures. These measures define the conditions that will exist upon successful completion. The subordinate and his or her manager agree to *written* objectives with *written* measures of quality, quantity and timeliness or cost. The employee controls his or her own performance once measures are written and agreed upon. The employee is given complete freedom to do all that is necessary to meet these objectives—and does. The subordinate and/or the manager use the measures to maintain control.

Blake and Mouton's Management Grid

Management consultants Robert R. Blake and Jane Srygley Mouton present management styles as a two-dimensional grid (see Figure 5.2). One axis measures an individual's degree of concern for production, the other measures concern for people. Each style on the grid embodies a belief about what motivates people.

The ideal style, according to Blake and Mouton, is one that shows a high degree of concern for both people and production. This style embodies the belief that there is no conflict between the two concerns. People can become involved in and

Figure 5.2   Blake and Mouton's Management Grid

```
(high)
C 9  1,9                                            9,9
o    People come first.          High concern for
n 8  ("Harmony is more           people and
c    important than              production.
e 7  results.")                  ("Everyone's a
r                                winner.")
n 6
                    5,5 Equal concern
f 5                 for people and
o                   production.
r 4                 ("Nobody wins or
                    loses.")
P
e 3  Neither people nor          Production comes
o    production are              first. ("Good guys
p 2  important. ("Don't          finish last.")
l    make waves.")
e 1  1,1                                            9,1
(low)

     1    2    3    4    5    6    7    8    9
   (low)              Concern for Production      (high)
```

committed to their work. The challenge is to develop a climate in which people will make this commitment.

The grid provides a motivational framework in another way. An employee's current beliefs will match one of the grid's quadrants. Determine which quadrant the employee is in and how to move him toward 9,9. A 1,1 is either retired or a bureaucrat. Show him that he can't succeed anymore by merely doing things "by the book." A 1,9 employee is terrified of conflict. Show him that it takes results for people to be truly satisfied. A 9,1 thinks only of numbers. Show him how many more numbers he'll have if he meets people's concerns.

Herzberg's Motivation-Hygiene Theory

Frederick Herzberg discovered what really motivates people. His interviews led him to conclude that factors such as money were not motivators at all. These "hygiene factors," while essential to worker satisfaction, did not provide positive motivation. They served only to prevent *dis*satisfaction. In order of importance, the hygiene factors are company policy and administration, supervision, relationship with supervisor, work conditions, salary, relationship with peers, personal life, relationship with subordinates, status and security.

What then are the motivators? They are the factors that increase satisfaction from work and motivate superior effort and performance. *Achievement, recognition, work itself, responsibility, advancement and growth:* Without them there is no motivation. The challenge is to enlarge and enrich every employee's job so that the motivational factors can work. Hygiene factors should be addressed but not confused as motivators. No matter how much money an incentive program provides, it will not succeed unless it addresses the employee's needs for achievement, recognition, work itself, responsibility, advancement and growth.

• •

"To please is a great step towards persuading them."

LORD CHESTERFIELD, LETTERS TO HIS SON, *1739*

• •

Motivating New Employees—The Success Kit

Big Jim Miller, founder of the office supply dealership in Fort Worth, Texas, that bears his name, Miller Business Systems and Business Interiors, is a popular motivational speaker and a founding member of the Dallas CEO Club. His company has close to 500 employees and does in excess of $100 million in annual sales.

Miller believes the most important day in an employee's life is the first day of work, so he gives every new employee a Motivational Success Kit. It contains:

1. A pen that says "TERRIFIC." Miller asks his employees to say "terrific" because it is one of the ten points on the Million Dollar Certificate (see page x). The word "terrific" is uplifting and makes people feel good.
2. A mirror. The mirror says, "I believe in myself. . .the best is yet to come." It is important for employees and key management personnel to believe they are the best people for the job.
3. A bottle of enthusiasm. This has become Miller's trademark. Enthusiasm costs nothing and is extremely contagious. He will refill your bottle free anytime.
4. A piece of string. If you try to push a piece of string in a straight line, it coils and resists. If you lead it and pull it, it will follow. The lesson to be learned from this piece of string is that you employ people who are leaders, people who will lead by direction rather than push for results.
5. A copy of a poem titled "The Man in the Glass." The poem imparts a positive philosophy about life and fellow human beings:

The Man in the Glass

When you get what you want in your struggle for self
and the world makes you king for a day
Just go to a mirror and look at yourself
and see what THAT man has to say.
For it isn't your father, mother or wife
Whose judgment upon you must pass;
The fellow whose verdict counts most in your life,
Is the one staring back from the glass.
Some people may think you a straight-shooting chum
And call you a wonderful guy,
But the man in the glass says you're only a bum—
If you can't look him straight in the eye.
He's the fellow to please—never mind all the rest,
for he's with you clear up to the end.
And you've passed your most dangerous, difficult test
If the man in the glass is your friend.

You may fool the whole world down the pathway of life
And get pats on your back as you pass,
But your final reward will be heartaches and tears—
If you've cheated the man in the glass!
Author Unknown

Miller encourages employees to follow the ten steps listed on the Million Dollar Certificate. In doing so, they will feel like a million, and so will everyone they come in contact with.

Employees Forever

Jim Miller understands the high cost of employee turnover. He notes that "With all the sophisticated computer hardware and software programs on the market today, no one has been able to adequately reflect the cost of employee turnover on a monthly balance sheet." He suggests several actions your company can take to reduce employee turnover and thereby increase profit:

1. Send a welcome letter to the homes of new employees before they begin their career with your firm. Welcome them, not as corporate employees but as members of your family. Tell them that you and the company are glad they are part of the team.
2. Think of an employee's first day on the job as "Employee's Day." On this day, spend a lot of time with the person on orientation. Review your employee handbook thoroughly so he or she will have a better understanding of what your company is all about. Have someone in the department take the new person to lunch, and assign someone to be a "buddy" for the first month. A buddy helps the new employee adjust and feel comfortable during the training period. It is essential for the new employee to feel accepted the very first day on the job.
3. Send thank-you letters to employees when they have done a job over and above the norm. Mail these letters directly to their homes so they can share them with family and friends.

4. Send employees a personalized birthday card.

You have to strive to reduce employee turnover. While it does not show up on a balance sheet, it is a very expensive part of doing business.

Reward Small Accomplishments

There is no such thing as a small accomplishment. There is only an accomplishment that hasn't been properly recognized. Did you ever notice that some parents put up a Welcome Home sign when their children have been away for a while? Doesn't that make you feel warm? In the Jewish religion, when a child reaches puberty, the family arranges a bar mitzvah to welcome the child into adulthood. In a similar vein, Jim Miller offers a celebration on the most stressful day for a new employee—the first day on the job.

So motivation is a force that comes from within, and it's your job as a rainmaker to tap that force. Remember, your employees will do what you *expect* if you remember to *inspect* what they do, with *respect*.

6 *Entrepreneurial Persuaders versus Con Artists*

"Cheat me in price, but not in the goods I purchase."

SPANISH PROVERB

Again, I do not condone or encourage their behavior, but I find that most, not all, rainmakers at certain times are indistinguishable from a "con."

One person in history seems to have successfully straddled both camps: the legendary Phineas Taylor Barnum, one of the founders of the Barnum and Bailey Circus. His other legacy is the saying: "There is a sucker born every minute." This statement has stood the test of time.

If you think the modern day con will not be viewed by history as a Robin Hood, odds are you are naive. If you're ever in Bridgeport, Connecticut, go to 820 Main Street to a three- story, Victorian brownstone museum. Can you guess who was mayor of this southern Connecticut town from 1875–76, and who is the hero of this museum? I'll give you a hint—he also gave the world "the greatest show on earth." Yes, we have a serious museum dedicated to P.T. Barnum, and it draws crowds every day. Once when I visited with my family I thought I saw P.T. outside scalping theater tickets, but it might have been done with mirrors. You never can be sure, and that's why a sucker is born every minute.

In his day, P.T. was a rainmaker. Con men and rainmakers both use those principles, but as Professor Vesper says, only one of them uses them to create real value.

So "cons" and entrepreneurs should be judged by the eyes of the sucker. Enough said.

Following are three basic traits of human behavior that everyone who persuades uses, whether "con" or not.

1. the Pygmalion effect
2. the jelly bean principle
3. the length of pieces of string

The Pygmalion Effect

When it comes to hiring help, there are two schools of thought. The first says "Let's automate everything and hire unskilled, low-paid people for everything else." Many entrepreneurs go this route in the early stages of company development, figuring that it will keep costs down. But before long they see that they can't get quality work.

The second school of thought starts out with good people and pays them good salaries from the beginning. I agree with that approach.

I have concluded that you don't motivate employees—they motivate themselves. As a manager, your job is not to demotivate them. Rainmakers select only motivated employees as the single best method of improving their firms' performance. (See Chapter 5 on motivational theories.)

A fascinating piece of behavioral research, conducted by two Harvard doctoral candidates in the field of education, is called the Pygmalion, or "late bloomer" effect. Here's how it was conducted.

All the fourth grade pupils in the San Francisco, California, public schools were asked to take an I.Q. test. The researchers then sent a personal letter to a random selection of fourth grade teachers. The letter was short, personal and to the point. In essence, it said:

Johnny Jones, who is in your class, is probably not performing at his full potential, according to our testing. We see strong signs that Johnny may be a genius but that he also appears to be a late bloomer. We judged it best to alert you to this finding, but we suggest you don't share the information with anyone until a future determination can be conducted.

Each letter was typed and personally signed.

One year later, these students, who were fictitiously labeled late bloomers, were tested again, and their performance was analyzed against the performance of the group as a whole. I don't really need to tell you the results, do I? The study wouldn't be worth relating to you unless the change was significant. And it was!

The message here is that of the self-fulfilling prophecy. When someone young enough to develop is given small signs of encouragement, great developments can occur. The power of words of encouragement toward your younger employees can be staggering. You can actually improve their performance simply by raising your expectations about their possibilities. If you think they are good and communicate this to them, they just might become good.

Here's another entrepreneurial persuasion technique, called the placebo effect. Most of us are aware of this phenomenon. People who are told a drug will have a certain effect will many times experience that effect, even when given an empty pill with no active properties. Norman Cousins, who learned first-hand the power of belief in eliminating his own illness, concludes, "Drugs are not always necessary. Belief in recovery always is."

The Jelly Bean Principle

The jelly bean principle explains why entrepreneurs and financiers seldom see events in the same perspective. I came up with this principle when I decided to run a little experiment during one of my seminars for entrepreneurs and bankers.

During lunch, I brought out a big glass jar filled with red jelly beans. I placed it next to the podium on a little table. I then pointed out the window to a black Mercedes parked on the street below and announced that the car would be awarded to the person who could guess *exactly* how many jelly beans were in the jar. The person whose guess was the closest would not receive a prize.

I did this in both the entrepreneurs and the bankers seminars. Each person was given one guess, which they wrote on a piece of paper. Both entrepreneurs and bankers took about the same amount of time to guess. They all eyed the jelly bean jar, picked it up and felt its weight. The distribution of guesses in both groups was a bell-shaped curve, with 1,000 as the mean. For both groups, the guesses looked roughly like this: 1,101; 886, 1,161; 1,211; 547; 1,762; 671; 981; 1,662; 666; 1,865; 786; 630; 455; 1,331; 1,470; 1,541; 1,030.

After the initial guesses were all written on the blackboard, I moaned it was such a shame not to be able to give away that wonderful car. (I sometimes struggled with the ethical question of what I would do if someone actually guessed correctly: Would I eat one jelly bean or give away a stranger's car? Is that a con?) I enthusiastically announced a second round of guesses, with the car going to the person who came closest. This got everyone's attention.

In the first round, both the bankers and the entrepreneurs made guesses that formed a bell-shaped curve. In the second round, though, things changed dramatically. The bankers' curve narrowed until it formed an almost straight vertical line around the mean, which was 1,000. The entrepreneurs' curve, on the other hand, spread out horizontally until it was almost flat. In the second round, the bankers bunched up their guesses around the mean of the original distribution. Because there were no hard data to work with, they chose to create data, and they bunched (like turkey and sheep) their answers around an imputed norm, where it was safe and warm. The entrepreneurs made second guesses that ranged from 300 to 3,000. They all grabbed for their own share of turf, figuring that way they'd have a better chance of being the closest to the unknown figure.

The natural tension between bankers and entrepreneurs comes from the fact they are different psychological types. Entrepreneurs are driven by nature to strike out on their own, away from the pack, while bankers are driven to play it safe and minimize their losses. Each is in a different business because each is a different kind of person.

The Length of Pieces of String

Another experiment I did for bankers involved eight pieces of string. Seven pieces were 22 inches long, but the eighth piece was only 18 inches long. The strings were laid out on a table with one end of each aligned to the others so that everyone could clearly see that all the strings except the last one were the same length.

I then planted six stooges in the room. Actually they were entrepreneurs, but I made them wear nice three-piece suits so they looked like bankers. The stooges were instructed to say that the strings were all the same length. Then I brought in the subject, usually a financial type. After a few warm-up questions, I asked the subject if all the strings on the table were the same length. While he was thinking, I asked each stooge the same question. So what do you think this poor banker said after hearing his "peers" agree that the strings were the same length? Naturally, he concurred.

No matter how I did it, the results of the experiment were always the same. I tried it on a bunch of different bankers at the seminar and tried varying the number of stooges from two to eight. It didn't matter. When a banker heard more than one other person who he thought was a banker say the strings were the same length, he agreed.

The findings were fascinating, but the experiment was getting a little boring, so I devised a variation, sort of a "con" on a con. I told one of the stooges to say that he thought the eighth string was shorter. What do you know? Our banker suddenly became a hero, now that he had an ally! He said, "Hey, there's a short piece of string there!"

I concluded that *It's almost impossible to persuade someone of something that is not true if that person has one or more trusted allies for the truth.*

This string experiment tells a great deal about human behavior, and its applications are intuitively obvious to a great persuader. If one of a tribe's high-ranking braves loses faith in the rainmaker's dance, the chances of rain are greatly diminished. Smoke screens and mirages will only delay the downfall of the rainmaker because the die is cast when the heads of the hunting parties no longer believe.

As you have undoubtedly observed, I believe there is a little "con" in every persuader. To accomplish so much, to be a high achiever, often requires a persuader who creates double images or even mirages. They always use smoke screens. Persuaders often straddle the line between right and wrong in an all-out effort to make others see their vision.

But persuasion is not stealing. Persuasion is not lying. And entrepreneurial persuaders don't do either. A good card player doesn't need to cheat.

Cheating, lying and stealing are not fun, and they spoil the game. Yet, in most persuasion activities, where and how wide to draw the line is an individual choice. It involves creating mirages and smoke screens rather than lying or cheating. It's more challenging to create a mirage.

Not Telling All the Truth

One of the great movies of all time is *The Godfather*, part one. One scene involves a direct confrontation between the new Godfather, Michael Corleone, and his wife, Kay, over a central issue. One of the terrible deeds Michael had to do before assuming this new position of power was to execute his sister Connie's husband. Kay says, "Michael, you're a brute. How could you kill your own brother-in-law?" The new Don is confronted by an outraged wife who has seen through his charade. A mirage won't solve this one.

A persuader never considers surrender. Michael turns to his wife and shouts back: "Didn't we have an agreement not to discuss business? Didn't we have a full understanding that we would never, ever discuss business? Why are you violating that agreement?" And after he slams his fist on the desk, to emphasize this point, he says, "I will not have a violation of that agreement."

His wife takes a step back and repeats her question: "Michael, is it true?" He looks her in the eye and says, "O.K. This one time I'll let you ask me about my affairs." Then he looks her directly in the eye and says "No. That's all. Just *no!*" Then they hug in a tight embrace.

Author Mario Puzo implies that she was wrong to violate the first agreement and that Michael was wrong to lie. But he and director Francis Ford Coppola leave the viewer with the belief that two wrongs make a right, sometimes. That's a smoke screen, not a mirage.

This is not a book about ethics. Rather, it is about persuasion, or getting others to see your point of view, and that sometimes requires a level of deception. Rainmakers straddle the truth/deception interface and sometimes fall and stumble off on the wrong side.

As I mentioned earlier, I have written a monthly newsletter for almost 15 years. One of the topics that generated the most reader reaction was a commentary about the travel industry. Here is what we published and a response from a CEO Club rainmaker, Larry Klur, who judges that all entrepreneurial persuaders need not resort to dishonesty.

The Travel Industry

A few years ago, we published an extremely controversial suggestion from one of our members. She was disgusted with the room rates charged her when she traveled and stayed at hotels. In one case she was being charged $125 for a room, while the persons on both her left and right were being charged about one half that fee for the same room. She was furious but had little choice. Her three-person public relations agency did not qualify for the same group discounts allowed her fellow travelers. She grew to believe the travel industry was ripping off small businesspersons.

Her solution, which we reported in this newsletter, was an ethical nightmare. The next time, she called the hotel's banquet operation *before* she made her reservation, to uncover the name of the largest group then using the hotel. When she called back and registered for a room, she identified herself as part of the convention and received the lowest room rate.

When we published this a few years ago, we received more letters and phone calls than you can imagine. Three out of four of them were negative, judging her a liar and crook. We took the heat, and I wondered for a long while if we were wrong in publishing this material. Most reasoned that two wrongs don't make a right.

Last month the CEO Clubs speaker, Chuck Whitlock, suggested a market niching technique for the travel industry. It was one of a dozen examples, but again, it caused a commotion. Los Angeles CEO Club member Tony Bianco of Peerless Travel was infuriated.

What Whitlock suggested was a travel agent card for every small businessperson, to allow them to get travel agent prices and services. The card was a genuine travel agent card, and it cost $500.

Whitlock and others have sold hundreds, if not thousands, of these cards. These cards allow travel agents' rates at hotels and resorts, and they allow a good talker to upgrade to first class when the airplane seats are available. The question is, Are they also ethical? In my opinion, the travel industry has been ripping off the little guy for years, but I don't believe two wrongs make a right.

What follows is one of the many responses to this article*:

Dear Joe:

I've just received and read your October *Entrepreneurial Manager's Newsletter* and am quite disturbed with your article on the travel industry.

Parents cannot understand why their children turn out morally bankrupt when they have been exposed in their formative years to income tax evasion, keeping incorrect change from a storekeeper, not returning customers' overpayments . . . the list can go on and on. Likewise, business owners cannot understand why well-treated employees would steal from them.

Your article pussyfoots around the real answer: This is an illegal, immoral act that steals from airlines and hotels without using a gun. It is probably similar to the white-collar

---

*Reprinted by permission of Larry Klur, CEO, West Cabot Cosmetics.

crimes in your lead article on page 2. It is inconsistent that an employer should have their employees help defraud others but be honest in their dealing with the employer.

I believe that your tacit approval of this through listing the source for more information and covering your a-- by asking the reader to answer the "ethical question" is also inconsistent with the goals of this organization. I trust that all of your members seek continuing education, ideas on improving quality and profitability, personal growth, etc.—and not ideas on how to cheat without getting caught.

Joe, please continue to maintain the highest standards that you have demonstrated over the years. They have served you well in the past, and there's no reason to believe they won't continue to serve us well in the future.

Written with love,

Larry Klur, CEO
West Cabot Cosmetics
Central Islip, New York

And my response on September 30, 1991:

Dear Larry:

I personally appreciate your letter of September 24th and your views of ethics as discussed in my newsletter via the travel industry. I can say three definite things about the subject:

1. I'll reprint your letter in the next newsletter, as you are not alone in your opinion and I value your input.
2. Tony Bianco, the CEO of Peerless Travel and a member of the Los Angeles CEO Club, agrees 100 percent with you, and I've invited him to write about the alternative of the value of a good travel agent in the next newsletter.
3. In my 15 years of writing this newsletter, no subject has gotten more response than this one. Hands down. But hundreds of CEO Club and CEM members have proven their opinion by paying up to $500 for these and other travel cards. They disagree with you as evidenced by their pocketbooks.

On a personal scale, I don't use these cards although I can receive them free. I don't get any money in any way from the sale of the cards. Never have, never will. But I do think it proper to try to present the issue in the newsletter, as both sides have good arguments.

You are a gentleman and a scholar to share your opinion. Sincerely,

Joseph R. Mancuso
President

I don't offer you solutions, but the ethical balancing act necessary to agree with both sides in this travel industry debate requires skill at walking on a taut tightrope.

What Is Truth?

Do you recall the Senate confirmation of Supreme Court Justice Thomas? He had been accused of sexual harassment by tenured law professor Anita Hill. The televised hearings provided entertainment for the whole country on a slow news weekend.

All observers agreed on one point: Both sides could not be telling the truth. The country soon took sides for or against, and the Senate then voted that Clarence Thomas should be given a lifetime appointment while still in his forties to the U.S. Supreme Court. The vote was 52–48—the largest number of senators voting against a Supreme Court justice in history.

Could some senator have believed that Thomas was not telling all the truth (sometimes known as lying) and have still voted for him? Do you think that all 52 senators who voted to confirm him to the highest court in America all believed only his side of the story? Then you must always reexamine the issue of truth because there is a possibility that at least one senator voted to confirm to the U.S. Supreme Court someone he deemed to be a liar. Interesting, isn't it?

All Truths Are Not True

If you are having trouble with these "con"cepts about the rainmaker's ability to walk the tightrope between truth and lies, here is yet another way to think about it.

1. Did you know that in the famous movie, *Casablanca*, Humphrey Bogart never said "Play it again, Sam"?
2. Did you know that the astronomer Carl Sagan claims that he never said "billions and billions and billions of stars"?
3. Did you know that Sherlock Holmes never said "Elementary, my dear Watson, elementary"?
4. How many times have you pretended not to be calling from a touch-tone phone in order to avoid voice mail?
5. How many times have you heard of someone using a cable T.V. descrambler to get free viewing of premier channels?
6. A radar detector is illegal in many states, yet millions are sold every year.
7. How many parents lie about their address to allow their children to attend schools in another area than where they actually live?
8. Have you ever bought a gold chain, VCR or camcorder from a shady character hanging out on Canal Street in Manhattan? Do you really think he could be a legitimate distributor?
9. How many people "adjust" their primary residence to avoid taxes?
10. Do you know anyone who has tried to cheat the airlines by using a false name when flying, to accumulate frequent flyer miles? Or who faked a doctor's letter to get a refund on an airline ticket?

The list is endless, but I want to be clear that truth can include various shades of gray.

The Greatest Cons of Our Time*

I have chosen five famous—or infamous—men as the greatest cons of our time: Charles Ponzi, Chase Revel, J. David

---

*Parts of this section have been adapted (especially the discussion on Charles Ponzi) from Jerry Buchanan's *Info Marketing Report* ($195 per year), *Towers Club*, USA, Inc., P.O. Box 2038, Vancouver, WA 98668-2038.

Dominelli, Michael Milken and Ivan Boesky. Their money-making strategies are all grounded in the same basic principle: the "pyramid scheme."

The Pyramid Scheme

The pyramid scheme is just a variation of the familiar chain letter. According to the SEC, a typical pyramid plan works as follows: Promoter P offers A and B a chance to buy distributorship at $1,000 each, which will give them the "exclusive right" to sell distributorship to others for $1,000 each and to sell certain products or services to the public. Each $1,000 that A and B receive from their sales of distributorship must be divided with P, perhaps on a fifty-fifty basis. In theory, A and B can realize $500 on each distributorship that they sell and can completely recover their initial investment by selling only two each. Meanwhile, P not only receives $2,000 front money from A and B, but $2,000 more if each sells two distributorships, which in turn will sell other distributorships, and so on, ad infinitum. The number of investors needed to keep the scheme going is quickly surpassed, and it becomes a matter of millions of tail-enders trying to find new victims. Unfortunately, every other house on the block already has a distributor.

Charles Ponzi

Charles Ponzi, a five-foot, four-inch self-educated Italian immigrant, used the pyramid principle to defraud some 40,000 Bostonians out of $10 million in 1920. Ponzi had done time in both U.S. and Canadian prisons, where he learned about pyramid cons from other inmates. He studied how a youthful William F. Miller, nicknamed "520 Percent Miller," had taken $1 million from Brooklyn, New York, residents in 1901 by promising to invest the money in a surefire stock market scheme that would pay 10 percent profit a week, or 520 percent a year. Miller landed in prison, but his financial exploits became legendary.

Ponzi claimed to have a secret system for moving postage stamps from country to country in such a way that a stamp bought in one country for five cents was worth ten cents in another. Of course, there was no such system; it was just part of the "sting." Investors were promised a 50 percent profit in 45 days or a 200 percent profit in 90 days. The first investors actually did receive those returns, and, in a state of elation, they let their friends in on what they thought was a good thing.

The little promoter never had to resort to mail order or advertisements because his scheme was set up to work by word-of-mouth promotion from the first suckers. This was his refinement to the old pyramid con—to take the first money and reinvest it in the sting to get more and more investors in an ever-growing cascade. Once the operator had enough money, he would either file bankruptcy or head for a life of exile in Brazil.

Within six months, Ponzi had taken in about $20 million, and after paying half of it back to the original investors, he had more than $5 million in his own bank account. He lived like a millionaire and mixed with judges, bank presidents, police officials and celebrities such as Gentleman Jim Corbett. He was written about frequently in the papers, shown relaxing on a veranda at his mansion with his 20-year-old bride and his aging mother.

What happens to most Ponzi schemers also happened to Ponzi himself: The millions in his bank accounts went to his head. With money pouring in at the rate of $1 million a week, he began to believe that he might be able to invest the profits legitimately, pay off all the investors and still come out a rich man.

Then the *Boston Post* ran the story of his prison record along with the mug shots, and his house of cards collapsed. When investors stormed his offices demanding refunds, he tried to make them all but came up $3 million short. He was arrested, jailed and deported back to Italy.

He left behind several banks in total collapse, some local politicians ruined and a grieving wife who eventually divorced him. Ironically, it was the Securities and Exchange Commission (SEC) that prosecuted Ponzi because the "doing business as" name he had chosen was the Security and Exchange Company.

During his heyday, he was known as the "Wizard of Wall Street." What the "wizard" failed to learn from "520 Percent Miller" was that, clever as he was, Miller landed in prison.

Ponzi Clones

New Ponzi schemers continue to pop up with alarming regularity. In 1973, Joseph Ferdinando, an ex-meter reader for a New York utility company, claimed to be operating a company that was buying up bad debts from small companies and making the collections for a very large cut of the amount of the debt. Investors were to reap a huge and quick reward. Some of his suckers were actually members of the Queens district attorney's staff.

In 1974, Robert D. Johnson, a Virginia telephone company employee, was exposed after 20 years as a Ponzi operator. His scam was telling the investors that he was buying up "industrial wine" to sell to salad dressing companies. It finally was revealed that there is no such thing as industrial wine. Wine is either wine or it is vinegar. There is no in-between. Johnson promised 200 percent profit on the suckers' money and paid off often enough to keep the money rolling in for ten years.

The swindle of the century was uncovered in early 1975 when it was discovered that more than 3,000 investors (big names like Jack Benny, Barbra Streisand, Liza Minelli, Walter Matthau, Andy Williams and even Adam Smith, the Wall Street book author) had sunk more than $20 million into an oil-drilling scheme run by Home-Stake Production Co. That these people and thousands like them had given their cash to an unknown Oklahoma lawyer named Robert S. Trippet for nearly 20 years (Andy Williams alone put in $538,000) was a startling revelation. But more surprising was the fact that they were swindled, not by a complex system involving computers and stock manipulations, but by the best-known of all confidence rackets: the Ponzi scheme.

By now everybody knows the story about Georgia farm boy Glen Turner and his "Dare To Be Great" movement. It was another pyramid scheme, and Turner will spend the next two or three decades going back to court to fight his appeals and convictions.

Captain Money and the Golden Girl

Captain Money and the Golden Girl is the inside story of the "J. David affair"—a $200 million fantasy of love, power and greed in southern California. This engagingly written book by *San Diego Union* reporter Donald C. Bauder is the story of a modern-day Ponzi scheme, replete with power, sex and money. The villain is J. David "Jerry" Dominelli, a stockbroker, who told investors that he could earn 50 percent annual returns in the volatile foreign currency market. The color is provided by his lover, Nancy Hoover, a tall, vivacious liberal who played in high society. J. David was as ugly as she was beautiful, and she was also well connected. It's one of the best books of the 1980s.

The J. David & Company scam was certainly not nearly so big as the Bank of Credit and Commerce (BCCI) debacle. The 1,200 investors in the Dominelli deal lost just under $100 million around 1982—the same as fine paid by Ivan Boesky. Boesky got only a three-year prison sentence, Mike Milken got ten years, and poor Jerry Dominelli is currently serving a twenty-year federal prison term.

In hindsight, Jerry was penalized partially for the high life-style he attained and the beautiful women he attracted. It has been said that if he wasn't so ugly or not been in the southern California spotlight, he would have been treated better. That's one of the reasons I've chosen him as one of my three biggest cons.

Say It Ain't So, Chase Revel

Kate Barrett-Whitney claims that she lived with Chase Revel, the colorful Los Angeles-based founder of *Entrepreneur* magazine, in 1984 and 1985. (It's ironic that the magazine for entrepreneurs was founded by a "con." That's why I rank it among the all-time greats.) She says that she left Revel because he became abusive. Then she brought a multi-million-dollar palimony suit against him.

Revel denied abusing Barrett-Whitney and claimed that she was merely his housekeeper. Sounds like your average palimony case, with bitterness and acrimony. But there is an interesting twist. Along with the palimony suit, Barrett-Whitney and her lawyer brought out some surprising facts about Revel's early life as an entrepreneur.

Documents filed in connection with the palimony suit indicate that in the early days, Revel had a rather unconventional system for raising capital: He robbed banks! The story, which was explored at length in an August 1, 1986, article in the *Los Angeles Times*, goes like this.

About 20 years ago, Revel, who was then known by his given name, John Leonard Burke, went to the Texas Employment Commission to hire four men with cars. Claiming to be Charles Hudson, an electrical contractor specializing in wiring banks, he offered to pay them $2 an hour to collect his payrolls. Then, in a single morning, he sent the men to four specific tellers at specific Houston banks. Once at the teller's booth, they were to hand the teller a bag for the payroll and a sealed envelope. In each envelope was a note warning the teller that if he didn't fill the bag with money, the life of his son (who was mentioned by name) would be in jeopardy.

The result: One of his employees left the bank empty-handed when the teller he was supposed to see wasn't there. Another was arrested at the bank. A third came away with the $11,000 "payroll" and turned it over to Burke. And the fourth was arrested after leaving the bank with about $10,000.

Burke, who claimed to be a Las Vegas gossip columnist named Jacques Victor Baron, was subsequently arrested, convicted and sentenced to four years in prison. On being released, he settled in Los Angeles under the name of Rio Sabor and started a business called the Starving Artists Galleries. He claimed to be the world's largest retailer of oil paintings. Later, under the name of Jacques Victor Baron, he started a business named Aetna Express—"the west's most dependable shipping agents."

In 1972, Baron was indicted for mail fraud in connection with Aetna Express. He pleaded guilty and was placed on probation. When he resurfaced, Burke/Baron/Sabor had taken the name Chase Revel, and he was publishing the *Insider's Report* (a forerunner of *Entrepreneur* magazine) which, ironically, told of small business opportunities and exposed schemes designed to separate would-be entrepreneurs from their cash.

Revel seemed to have found his true calling. *Entrepreneur* magazine prospered (circulation is currently 500,000), and he went on to write books such as *184 Businesses Anyone Can Start and Make a Lot of Money* and *168 More Businesses Anyone Can Start and Make a Lot of Money*. His flamboyant lifestyle made him the subject of feature articles on starting small businesses in *The New York Times* and *The Wall Street Journal*.

But even before the palimony suit, things had begun to sour. In 1982, Chase Revel, Inc., which published *Entrepreneur* magazine, filed for Chapter 11 bankruptcy. (The magazine later became property of a public company.) Today, the magazine's new owners have made it a wonderful success, and they totally disassociate with the founder.*

Boesky and Milken

No doubt about it—*Den of Thieves* by *Wall Street Journal* Pulitzer Prize winner James B. Stewart is the best detailed account of a modern day con. It's the story of Ivan Boesky, Mike Milken, Marty Siegel and Dennis Levine. Four bigger crooks you couldn't know.

To make the book an even bigger seller, famous Harvard professor and lawyer Alan Dershowitz (who wrote *Chutzpah* and was the star of *Reversal of Fortune*, a movie about Claus Von Bulow) has attacked the book. Dershowitz is defending Milken in his appeal, and he ran a full-page ad saying the book was wrong. I respect Dershowitz, but he was wrong to publicize the book because his disclaimer was the single reason I bought it. After all, who wants to read the truth?

Stewart spins a tale of crime, punishment and the quest for power. He shows how Michael Milken, Ivan Boesky, Martin Siegel and Dennis Levine created a series of security scams that made other financial hustles look like amateur night. He brings us the full narrative of events, from the day that "small fish" Dennis Levine ($12.6 million in illegal profits) forged the first link in his insider trading circle, to the moment when junk

---

Venture, another magazine for entrepreneurs, folded a few years ago. It's rumored that investors, led by the colorful Arthur Lipper III, lost $13 million over ten years trying to make this magazine profitable.

bond king Michael Milken (who earned $550 million in a single year) finally fell—despite his retinue of loyal supporters and public relations wizards.

As *Winning with the Power of Persuasion* was going to its last edit, the story of the collapse of Robert Maxwell's empire was just breaking. Early indications were that it was a multi-billion-dollar scam. It's too soon to rank it among these favorites, but it has all the ingredients of a long-time "winner."

The Three Great Lies of Entrepreneurs

We all know three greatest lies in the world, or at least our localized version of them. Recognizing the phenomenon, I sought to uncover the three most popular entrepreneurial lies. Unpublished until now—or is that a lie?

1.   The check is in the mail.
2.   We have a computer problem.
3.   I am from the government, and I am here to help you.

• •

"If you can't convince them, confuse them."

HARRY TRUMAN

• •

Not all entrepreneurs play around the edge of the playing field. Ross Perot, for one, likes to say that he plays in the middle. Not all entrepreneurs work to stay in front of the law, but did you ever wonder why all the politicians in Washington are part of a "con"gress? Shouldn't they be part of a "pro"gress?

Is putting your foot in the water and then withdrawing it so fast that it doesn't get wet the same as always being dry? In the bestselling book, *Rising Sun*, Michael Crichton says subterfuge is a normal and accepted part of Japanese business. Getting caught is not.

In America, we like to believe in an ideal world where all profit is derived from noble goals. Our entrepreneurs are judged not only by the wealth and jobs they create but by their position on the playing field. And when they step in the water too long and get just a little wet, the system sends them to jail for ten years and humiliates them for others to see. Poor Michael Milken can't even wear his toupee in prison, and he created more rain than all the judges in America. It's not a matter of fair; it's just the way it is in America. As boxing promoter Don King says, "Only in America."

7

The Seven-Step Selling Process— and Other Guidelines for Persuaders

"Being creative is having something to sell, or knowing how to sell something, or having sold something."

PAULINE KAEL, THE CREATIVE BUSINESS, *1968*

What is the key ingredient to start a business? No, it's not money or enthusiasm or a good idea. It's a customer. It's the only ingredient that is both sufficient and necessary. When someone finally says "I'll buy that," a business begins.

But how do you get to that ultimate point? How do you turn your prospects into buyers? No subject in the field of management has been analyzed more with less impact than selling. Because of this, many models have sprung up. The one I like best is the seven-step selling process. I call it the entrepreneurial persuasion selling model.

The Seven-Step Selling Process

Step 1—Research
Step 2—Prospecting
Step 3—Approach and preheat
Step 4—Qualifying the buyer
Step 5—Presenting the product
Step 6—Handling objections
Step 7—Gaining commitment

Step 1: Research

Buy from versus Sell To

Nobody likes to be sold to. What Fred Smith of Federal Express did while raising money to start an industry was allow someone to participate in an opportunity. He did not sell *to*; he allowed the customer the privilege of buying *from*. In hindsight, I wish he had given me a chance to get a little of that early Federal Express stock. How about you?

Keep in mind this principle: Whenever you are selling to somebody, that person is going to resist you. If you hold open your hand and push outward on the other person's hand, the natural reaction is to push back. Pressure generates resistance.

Buying from is just the opposite. It generates assistance, not resistance. It generates opportunities and friendships. It's when two hands are joined and a handshake results.

Research takes the cold out of sales calls. It is the key to the entrepreneurial persuasion selling model. Research occurs at the beginning of the selling process and lays the foundation for what follows. When the foundation is weak, the building is suspect.

During the research phase, you need to discover the answers to the other six steps before they occur. When you skip the research, you have to hope that your preheat or your ability to handle objections will do the job. Hope is a poor substitute for research.

During research you need to answer the same questions sought after by all good journalists: Who, what, why, when and where? Here are a few questions that you need to answer in the selling process:

Who?	Team	What is their need?
Receptionist	Current Supplier	What is their
Executive		situation?
Secretary		What is their hot
Administrative	**What?**	button?
Assistant	What is their	What is their
Decision Maker	business?	financial ability?

When?	**Where?**	**Why?**
When to install?	Where is the competition?	Why are they confused?
When to implant?		
When to monitor?	Where are their markets?	Why are they unsure?
When to influence?		
When to call?	Where are they going?	Why are they in a hurry?
When to make an appointment?	Where have they been?	Why are they buying?
When to close?		
When to service?	Where is their niche?	Why are they using the competition?
When to deliver?		
When to bill?	Where is their expertise?	
When to get referrals?	Where is the hidden opportunity?	
When to get testimonials?		

Step 2: Prospecting

• •

"The hours we pass with happy prospects in view are more pleasing than those crowned with fruition."

OLIVER GOLDSMITH, THE HERMIT, *1764*

• •

For many products, prospecting or determining the most logical location for customers is the hardest part of the selling process. Once you find the right person, the product's benefits can gain the customer's interest. Prospecting is plain hard work, and there are no known shortcuts or easy methods to do it! This is especially true for intangible products (insurance, stocks and bonds or any services).

Step 3: Approach and Preheat

During the approach, two major actions should occur. First, a salesperson should reduce relationship tension. In other words, you and the customers should feel at ease. Selling is not you doing something to the customer, but a shared experience, in which you solve the customer's problem together. At the same time, the salesperson should build task tension by showing concern for the customer's needs, such as "I understand that you don't have a dishwasher. I understand that you need a new car. I understand. . . ." The task that needs to be accomplished creates task tension. Selling is not a totally social exchange. You are there to represent your products and services. The other person is there for the service or the product you offer.

Preheating during the approach can also help take the cold out of sales calls. This step includes awards, testimonials, articles and, most important of all, referrals—all designed to warm the client to your approach. Allow your current and past customers to brag for you. Preheat is not a computerized form letter. That's called direct mail. Preheating lets your customers help you sell other customers. When your approach begins with a referral, you are on your way to success.

As you approach your prospects, keep in mind that most decisions to do business are made during the first five minutes. Don't underestimate the power of an early bias for or against you. *You never get a second chance to make a first impression.*

• •

"The world belongs to the enthusiast who keeps cool."

WILLIAM MCFEE, CASUALS OF THE SEA, *1916*

• •

Step 4: Qualifying the Buyer

This is the "hot button," and it focuses on the reason the buyer will eventually buy. Every product or service has several

salient features and attributes. Some of them are more important to certain customers than others. Not everyone buys the
same product for the same reason. The objective of step 4 is to
determine what turns the specific customer on. What button
do you push to get the order? What does the customer need?
This can be gained only through a careful questioning of the
customer. During step 4, you must probe, discover and question (PDQ) to determine the dominant buying motive (DBM). I
like to call it the *hot button.*

Step 5: Presenting the Product

Within this sales model, most sales personnel do this step
best. They are so familiar with their product, having presented
it numerous times, that they can usually make a convincing presentation about its features and benefits. The only issue here is
to stress the *benefits*, which are the perceived value the customer receives from the product, versus its features, which explain how your product is made or functions. Because most
salespeople do this so well, I won't dwell on it.

Step 6: Handling Objections: Feel, Felt, Found

. . . .

*"If there are obstacles, the shortest line between
two points may be the crooked line."*

BERTOLT BRECHT, GALILEO

. . . .

After the product has been presented, there will undoubtedly
be some objections, attempts to postpone purchase or discussion of the weaknesses of your product. How do you handle
these objections? The key is to avoid conflict—to frame things
so that a person is doing what he or she wants to do, not what
you want. It's very hard to overcome resistance. It's much easier

to avoid it by building on agreement. I call this the "feel, felt, found" approach, and here's how it works:

1. *Listen*. Don't interrupt; get the full objection before you respond.
2. *Cushion or acknowledge it*. Objections are not usually foolish, so empathize with the person and try to legitimize his or her feelings. Acknowledge that others have had similar objections. In fact, you can say that you understand how they *feel* and that others have *felt* that way, too.
3. *Question*. Remember, asking is the key to persuading. To handle an objection, you must unearth its source. Only then can you explain it away.
4. *Answer*. The first three steps focus on validating and understanding objections. Step 4 focuses on turning the negative aspects into positive answers. This is done by introducing new information. You might say something like this: "You are really only partially informed. We have *found* some new evidence that will put your mind to rest about our products." Customers are never wrong, but sometimes they are only partially informed. It's your job to supply the missing, pivotal information. The object is to spin the objection around and to use the power of the problem to be the power behind your persuasive answer.
5. *Confirm*. Be sure to confirm what you said is what was heard. Ask prospects to repeat what was just said to be sure they got it. It helps to program what you just said into their brain. When they repeat, they begin to accept what you have said. "Do you see any good business reason that we shouldn't start today?" is a confirmation of an objection that has been spun around and is now the reason to buy. Don't give them a chance, just a choice. "Can we do business now, or do I need to tell you more about it?" is another way to confirm.

The secret to your success is in how you handle those objections. Answer each question carefully. The goal is to reduce the risk to zero. To do this you need to learn to take an objection and turn it around so that it works for you instead of against you. I recommend the "feel, felt, found" technique.

Here's another way to handle objections. Let's say that a woman is out to buy a new dress because she and her husband are going to entertain a couple whom they haven't seen in some time.

While she is walking through the dress section at Bloomingdale's, she spots an ideal dress on a mannequin and asks the salesperson if it's available in her size. Then she goes to the changing rooms to try it on.

As she walks out on the way to the mirror, the salesperson remarks: "Don't you look fabulous in that dress!" The woman stands in front of the mirror, turns several times and notices that she does look quite good in this dress. As she leaves the mirror, she turns to the salesclerk and says, "If my husband doesn't like it, can I bring it back for a full refund?" And the answer at all good dress shops is "Absolutely! That's the way our company does business." Dress shops learned long ago that if they didn't offer a refund, no one would buy. It's a way of handling objections. So the salesperson boxes it up, and the woman brings it home.

The husband usually arrives home from work at around six o'clock. The wife asks herself: "Do we eat first or show him the dress first? Do I show him the dress in the box, or do I model it?"

People who have been married a long time will realize that a better decision can be made on a full stomach and that if they themselves needed to wear the garment to make a decision, why should they deprive their spouse of the chance to see it at its highest and best use? The newly married who fail to discover this natural law seldom remain married.

After dinner, while he is watching the evening news, the wife puts on the new dress. "How do you like it?" she asks.

The husband's response to that question is guaranteed in all marriages, new and old alike: "How much did it cost?"

That's the objection. Now, depending on the length of the marriage, different responses occur. Those who are newly married will immediately reveal the price. Those married a little longer will say "I saved you over four hundred dollars on this dress, as it was on a mark-down special." Those married the longest know better than to answer the objection. They just ignore it.

When he asks again or balks at the price, those who are married with children reply by saying, "You know this dress is magical. If you hang it properly in the closet, it never needs cleaning or ironing. Number two, this is a multiseasonal dress—it can be worn summer, fall, winter and spring. Number three, it's a multipurpose dress. Not only can I wear it to our evening dinner; I can also wear it around the house while I'm vacuuming and cleaning. And number four, it happens to be your mother's size and she said that she would use it when I'm not wearing it." Those four responses literally destroy the objection by shattering it with a sledgehammer!

Step 7: Gaining Commitment

This has traditionally been classified as the most important sales step, but it is not. Actually, the most vital sales step is qualifying the buyer (step 3). If that is completed properly and the approach is done properly, gaining commitment is the smallest and least stressful step in the entire selling process. To gain commitment, you may want to create an opportunity to close on an objection. Many objections can be handled by exercising the feel, felt, found technique. It's called a "trial close."

Sometimes salespeople enjoy the selling process so much that they go past the close and keep presenting the product rather than stopping to make the sale. For instance, suppose a customer is buying a house and likes everything about it but the location. You can't do anything about that, so you are not going to make the sale, and you must realize that. If, on the other hand, the objection occurs because the house has no fireplace and the customer continues to hang on that issue, don't make the mistake of saying, "You don't need a fireplace in today's society; a fireplace takes up the heat," or "it's a poor energy choice," or whatever.

Rather, you should acknowledge whatever the customer really wants. If a fireplace is important, accept the conclusion. The way to close on an objection is to say, "Do you like the location? Do you like the house? Is the price okay?" If the answer is yes, you can say, "You mean you would buy this house if it had a fireplace?" If the customer says yes, you only have to negotiate the price of the fireplace,and you have gained commitment.

Selling is the art of reaching agreement and building trust. The professional salesperson is an artist with a keen set of listening skills and an inner desire to perform. *The whole world is your customer, and you're selling every day to everyone—so why not get good at it?*

Models like the one outlined in this chapter are useful to a degree, but they are only models. A practicing salesperson also needs to know some basic principles of persuasion that are grounded in experience. Following are several such principles.

Pareto's 80/20 Philosophy

No concept in selling is more powerful than the Pareto Principle. It is wonderfully simple, and, in my view, it is more useful and accurate than systems that classify buyers and sellers into different types. Although it was discovered during the ancient civilizations in Rome and Greece, the 80/20 rule was popularized in the eighteenth century by the Italian philosopher, Pareto. It means that 80 percent of sales are made by 20 percent of the people. To view the principle from a buyer's point of view, consider that 80 percent of all products bought are purchased by 20 percent of the buyers.

And you may also think of 80/20 as a reminder that 80 percent of the successes you enjoy come from 20 percent of your activities, or that 80 percent of all problems in a company are caused by 20 percent of the employees. Feel free to add to this formula. But whatever you do to make it meaningful to you, write out the details of your 80/20 descriptions.

The point of all this is to remind you that a few people are usually responsible for most of what happens. If it is true that 80 percent of all business is done by 20 percent of all the people, it is very important that you not waste your time with the 80 percent who do only 20 percent of the business! When you combine two or more of these Pareto principles, you can really begin to focus your efforts.

Believability, Likeability and Trust

A second idea that has stood the test of time is the concept of *b*elievability, *l*ikeability and *t*rust (BLT). It too is simple: People buy only from other people who have BLT. Persuasion is the art of building trust and confidence. Trust is built by doing what you say you will do. It's not complicated; it's just hard to do.

Combine BLT with Pareto's 80/20 and you have a useful formula for selling:

1. Be *agreeable*. Always smile and be happy.
2. Give others the *attention* they need. Hold the spotlight on them, not you.
3. Make others feel *admired*. Talk about them, not about you.
4. Make others feel *appreciated*. Don't forget to say "thank you."
5. Make others feel *accepted*. Never put someone down.
6. Make others feel *approved*. He who judges is judged.
7. Give others *cooperation* and *help*. This creates friendship instead of resistance.
8. Make others feel *important*. Help them accomplish their goals, not yours.
9. Make others feel *needed*. Be vulnerable and allow them to help you.
10. Make others feel you *trust* them. It's a two-way street.
11. *Bonus* method: Don't be ashamed to say, "If you'll give me 5 percent of your trust to start, I'll earn the remaining 95 percent."

When Is the Best Time To Sell?

The best time to sell is immediately after you've sold. The theory behind this phenomenon, which is generally well accepted by practicing persuaders, is founded in psychological research conducted by Dr. Leon Festinger of Columbia University in the late 1950s. The research comes under the fancy academic name of *cognitive dissonance*. Cognitive dissonance is one of the most popular areas of academic inquiry within the marketing profession, as evidenced by the popularity of marketing doctoral dissertations on the subject.

Cognitive means being aware, and *dissonance* means being stressed. Together, the terms mean being aware of internal stress. Every individual who makes a difficult decision, including purchasing decisions, suffers from cognitive dissonance. When the cognitive dissonance reaches an intolerable level, the individual will take action to reduce the dissonance and return to equilibrium and harmony. What action does an individual take to reduce dissonance? Let us look at an example of an automobile buyer.

Creating Dissonance

You decide to buy one of the three popular American medium-sized cars. On a Saturday, you rush first to the Ford dealership, then across the street to the Chevy dealership and eventually down the street to the Plymouth dealership. Being a concerned buyer, you compare the features and prices of each car, but after a full day of comparison, you are still undecided on the best value. Finally, as the day wears on and your need for a car increases, you make a commitment with one of the three car dealers—the one you trust. For you, it was a difficult decision.

Have you ever wondered if the salesperson actually went to the back room for a final approval of your below-cost deal, or did he or she just go to the washroom while you wait in hope that the low price is agreeable?

This process occurs every day, and because 10 million new cars are sold annually under this back-and-forth dissonance-creating method, many of us have experienced it. Yet we all claim to have secured a "good deal" when we buy a new car. I don't know anyone who has ever admitted to a "bad deal," do you?

Dissonance Reduction

This new car decision-making process is known as a stress decision because, when it concludes, the purchaser's dissonance is very high. Consequently, when you bring the new car home, you will take the following steps to reduce that dissonance and justify your purchase.

1. You may inadvertently choose to leave the new car in your driveway rather than the garage or to drive and park it where it will be conspicuous to your neighbors.
2. The night you bring the car home, you will probably read the owner's manual and begin searching for new information about what a wonderful car you have chosen. You probably will never read the manual again, and you will either lose it or bury it in the glove compartment.
3. You will become extremely receptive to advertisements about the car you just purchased. You will ignore other automobile ads. That car will become the single most exciting thing for you for a period of time. You will reject the chance to read other automobile advertisements, preferring only to read those that reinforce the benefits of your car. Because car manufacturers are aware of your dissonance, the president of General Motors will send you a personal letter congratulating you on your wise choice. The company will also send you numerous questionnaires seeking feedback on the purchasing process. They'll also want to know how you like your car.

Besides providing useful information to car companies (actually, they can get this information through less costly sampling techniques), the questionnaire allows the buyer to vent any residual dissonance.

So the message is simple. The best time to sell is immediately after you've sold. The best time to make a sales call is immediately after you've made the sale. The best time to send a sales message is immediately after you've made a sale. That finding is built on Leon Festinger's concept of cognitive dissonance, and it works.

Many companies have built their marketing programs around dissonance reduction. Dissonance-reducing literature is enclosed in the dissonance-reducing product's shipping carton, which is appropriately marked to inform your peers, who may glance at it, that you made a wise choice. Wouldn't it be nice to have the salesperson who recently sold you the whatever pop in on you one week after you bought it? Isn't that a winning strategy? Entrepreneurial persuaders do it naturally.

New York CEO Club member Bruce Bendell, who owns and operates one of America's largest car dealerships—Major Automotive (located in Long Island City, New York)—sends one red rose to all owners of a new car purchased at Major. It's a nice touch and a way to say thank you. It also builds on this concept of cognitive dissonance. He used to send the rose to the new car owner's home, but now he sends it to the office. Why? It causes a great deal of discussion, and it has become the source of excellent prospects for his 35-person sales force. When someone asks about the rose at work, it often leads to a referral.

• •

"You can't sweep other people off their feet if you can't be swept off your own."

CLARENCE DAY, THE CROW'S NEST, *1921*

• •

What Is the Best Time of Day To Sell?

Seventy percent of all commercial sales are made between 7:00 A.M. and 1:00 P.M. I estimate that 70 percent of all direct sales and acts of persuasion or decision making occur during these six hours, which include two meal periods. Here is how Walter Hailey explains it:

Early in my career, I noticed that most of the rich and successful people seem to get up early and usually get off to a fast start. They get up earlier than most. Don't ask me why, because I really don't know the answer. But what is important to them should be important to you. If you are going to do business with these people, you need to see them early.

I recall during the years I was selling millions of dollars of insurance that I would see my prospects as early as seven in the morning. We would meet for breakfast or coffee. Some mornings I would have three different breakfast meetings!

One at 6:30, one at 7:30 and the third one at 9:00. Then I would see people for coffee until lunch time, and I would usually have lunch with a new client or prospect. Most of my sales were signed, sealed and delivered by early afternoon. That left the rest of the day for planning, paperwork and whatever.

Hailey warns against falling into the trap of sleeping until seven or eight and getting to your office at nine; then wasting time having coffee with your office buddies, who aren't going to buy anything from you anyway; then reading the paper and having a second cup of coffee. By then, it's time for lunch, and what has been accomplished? Very little. By 1 P.M., when 70 percent or more of the daily business has already been done, you have accomplished very little, if anything.

Hailey also warns against coffeepot seminars in the office. He says offices are usually good places for people to hide and feel like they are at work. He calls it the "fireman's syndrome." They wait until the bell rings, and then they go on a call. Trouble is, he concludes, "The bell doesn't ring much."

Hailey continues: "The nonproductive person (I avoid referring to them as 'workers,' but I can hardly think of them as 'salespeople') may pick up the phone and start making calls later in the day. If they are not able to write many orders, they should not be surprised. They are trying to work in a time period when little business is done and few sales are closed."

When sharpening your persuasive skills, remember the 7–1 principle. The people you call on will be most receptive early in the day. Hailey learned to call on his best executive prospects bright and early. "They are usually in their offices between 7:00 and 7:30 A.M., and they tend to answer their phone because the secretary has not arrived. It's quiet in their offices, and they have time to listen to your ideas." To prove his point, Hailey says that he has sold more than $500 million worth of life insurance before 10:00 A.M.

To accomplish this feat, he had many three-breakfast mornings. "It wasn't too hard," he says. "At the first breakfast meeting, I would have juice and coffee while my prospect had a complete breakfast. I had more time to talk and sell when I had less to eat. At the next breakfast, I would have a small meal, and at the third, it would be coffee and juice again. When you plan ahead, you can have several breakfast or lunch meetings and not overeat. And breakfast is a lot cheaper than dinner."

When I began as a consultant at the age of 23, I worked along Boston's famous Route #128 golden highway. My business was called Applied Marketing, and my letterhead had a rising sun intertwined with the A.M. logo. I used to tell my clients I liked the A.M. better than the P.M., and I almost always had breakfast (seldom dinner) meetings with my clients. I did that for seven years, and I came to believe in the value of getting a quick start out of the morning gate.

"What the Hell" Calls

Now that we agree that most sales occur during the early hours of the day, does that mean that you should take the afternoon off? Many salespeople do, and they make a big mistake. Although the early bird gets more worms in nonretail selling, most retail sales occur in the afternoon and evening.

You'll discover the best salespeople out selling in the morning when many companies are holding sales meetings. Doesn't that strike you as strange? Many successful salespeople settle into a situation after a while, and they relax and do paperwork in the afternoon. The eager beaver takes advantage of the lack of talent out in the afternoon and has developed a "what the hell" sales call.

Big Jim Miller popularized this phenomenon. Jim is a lifetime member and founder of the CEO Club of Dallas and the author of a wonderfully motivational business book, titled *The Corporate Coach*.

He tells the story of a rainy day and the decision to call it quits for the day by one of his salespeople. Having made a dozen or so calls in an office park with Big Jim, her hair was wet and straight and all her makeup was gone. Normally a very attractive person, she had become embarrassed by her appearance. As she and Jim were leaving the office park around 4:00 P.M. to go back to their office, they went past a parking lot filled with cars. Even without an appointment, Jim said, "Why can't we do just one more call on this company?" Even at the age of

60, Big Jim enjoyed selling and was proud of building a service business within a highly competitive industry. She replied, "Oh, I just can't go in. I look awful, and it's almost closing time for them."

Now we revisit the question of what is truth as Jim the Persuader looked at her and said, "Gosh, I personally think you look better with the natural look. You're naturally attractive, and to me you are now at your peak. What do you say? It'll take only a few minutes." Would you guess there was an element of the con in this statement? If you think so, you are wrong. To Big Jim she looked great, and I think he really meant it.

This customer eventually turned out to be one of Miller Business Systems' largest customers, and this salesperson now works only the late shift making "what the hell" calls. She likes to say, "What the hell do you have to lose by making this call?"

How Many Times Should You Call?

• •

"Nothing great was ever achieved without enthusiasm."

EMERSON, CIRCLES, *1841*

• •

The typical salesperson must call on a prospect four times before 20 percent of the buyers will say yes. After eight calls, 50 percent will buy; after a dozen calls, 70 percent will buy; and after fifteen calls, 90 percent of those called on will buy. The number fifteen is at the apex; it never gets any better than that. The message is simple: You can't sell them all.

The problem is that 80 percent of all salespeople quit after the first, second or third call—right when the odds are increasing that a sale will be made. The data indicate that 80 percent of all sales are made after the fifth call but that 80 percent of all salespeople quit after the fourth attempt.

These same principles apply in daily life. In fund-raising, 20 percent will give after being called on four times. After fifteen calls, 90 percent will have given. Walter Hailey says that he learned this from having spent 30 years calling on prospects. I verified the concept with academics and other sales persuaders. Of course, it varies by product, but the notion that salespeople quit calling too soon is well founded.

Hailey cautions that you should have a reason for making each sales call. He doesn't believe a salesperson should make calls just for the sake of making calls. You can quickly wear out your welcome after several calls saying, "I was just in the neighborhood and thought I would drop in to see if you are ready to buy." Of course, even this approach will work sometimes but not enough to keep your prospects looking forward to your call.

Make your clients and prospects happy to see you. Think of a new idea to share with them; some news about the industry that will interest them; some important or unique use of an existing product that they might not be aware of. This is where being creative pays off. The alert salesperson is always on the lookout for a fresh new twist that will get a client's attention and create goodwill.

The Difference Between Marketing and Selling

The difference between a marketing versus sales orientation can be determined partially by how you handle the subtle difference between a product's features and its corresponding customer benefits. Marketing is a customer looking for a product, whereas selling is a product looking for a customer. It's the same transaction, but it's either going forward or backward (see Figure 7.1).

An example of this distinction is highlighted in the quarter-inch drill story. An estimated 3,250,000 quarter-inch drills were sold in this country last year, which means that customers also bought 3,250,000 quarter-inch holes that year. It just happened that the drill was necessary to produce the hole. If anyone is ever able to package a hole, customers would begin buying the holes to solve their problem.

Figure 7.1   Marketing versus Sales Diagram

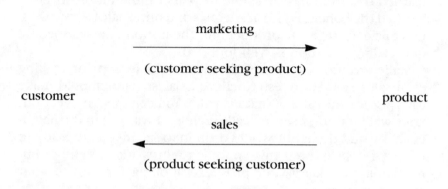

Product	Feature	Benefit
cosmetics	special fragrance	hope
drill bits	characteristics of drill	hole
encyclopedia	volumes of information	knowledge
computers	accounts receivable	management information systems

Charles Revson, the entrepreneur founder of Revlon, the famous cosmetics company, once expressed the same thing in another way. He said, "In my factory we make cosmetics, but in my stores we sell hope." Customers buy benefits, while you make features. *A customer benefit is a product feature turned inside out.*

8 *Finding a Market Niche*

"Babe Ruth made a big mistake when he gave up pitching."

TRIS SPEAKER, BASEBALL, *1921*

Think small—that's the advice I've often given to entrepreneurs. By finding a slice of the market that's been ignored because it seems too small, you can often turn out a profitable niche for yourself with minimum marketing effort and expense. Persuaders like niches better because they are often less competitive. What are some secrets to identifying and exploiting market niches?

Look for a market that's growing rapidly, and try to identify a portion of it that's being neglected. For example, one of the fastest-growing markets in the United States is videotape rentals. In New York City alone, hundreds of video stores have sprung up in the past few years. Ninety-nine percent of the VCRs currently being sold are VHS, so hundreds of entrepreneurs are slugging it out for a share of the market. However, 10 percent of existing VCRs are beta, and this market is underserviced. A "beta only" store (and as far as I can tell, there are only two currently in New York City) offers a doubly inviting niche: The market is out there just waiting to be tapped, and it's small enough that one or two outlets could easily control it without inviting competition. It's not a gold mine but a profitable small business.

Defining the market is crucial. I can't tell you how often I've heard that the potential market for someone's product or idea was "every man, woman and child." The funny thing is, I've never seen one of these products make it to market. This kind of thinking means that the market hasn't been defined. It's better to find an existing need and fill it than to work in an undefined market.

Tom Drewes, president of Quality Books in Lake Bluff, Illinois, has done just that. His company distributes books by small publishers to the library market. "Libraries are a $2-billion market," he says, "and most of that market is covered by the large wholesalers and the publishers themselves." Drewes estimates that as little as $1/10$ of 1 percent of sales to libraries are small press books. That's a mighty small niche, but it's worth millions a year to his company. And "while the publishing market is growing incrementally," Drewes says, "our company is growing like wildfire. Sales have gone up 20 percent, and profits have increased 100 percent in the last year."

Price alone isn't a niche. If all you offer is a cheap price, then someone else is going to come along and knock you off. Consider the personal computer market. A quick glance at any computer magazine will show you that there are dozens of mail-order companies selling no-name IBM PC clones at rock-bottom prices. Twenty small companies competing for the low end of the market hardly qualify as a niche. However, mail-order companies like Dell Corporation have created a niche as they eliminate or reduce margins for retailers.

Once you've got a niche, service the hell out of it. When you've got a good niche, you'll get business just by being there. If you don't do a good job, your customers might look elsewhere, but if you service it well, you might find yourself with a permanent niche.

Here's Drewes' approach: "We listen to our customers. We sell millions of books—one at a time. That requires patience and hard work, and maybe that's why no one else has come into the market to compete with us directly." That keeps the niche attractive.

The Product Life Cycle

Be aware of your product's life cycle. The life of a product or a service has four phases: (1) start-up, (2) growth, (3) maturity and (4) decline. At the start-up phase the market hasn't yet developed, so the chance of finding a viable niche is limited. In the growth stage the market is blossoming with niches. When the market reaches the mature stage, the niches tend to diminish. But niches sometimes reappear when a product's life cycle begins its decline. In fact, they occur whenever significant change occurs in the market structure. When the slope of the life cycle curve changes rapidly, that change creates niches.

Don't get too comfortable. A successful niche doesn't last forever. Markets change as do customers' needs and attitudes. Keep your eye on your own market, and on other markets, for opportunities. And be prepared to make changes if you see the market beginning to dwindle. One percent of a thriving market can be very profitable; 5 percent of a fading market can leave you awash in red ink.

Market Strategy—Think Small

Developing a marketing strategy is one of the more elusive procedures within the marketing discipline, especially for smaller, less well-heeled companies. A clever strategy, which is traditionally discussed under the umbrella title "Think Small," was what David needed to defeat Goliath. A simplified example serves the point better than a statement of what it means.

In the early 1970s, the ten major soap manufacturers were investigating the market for a soap concentrate for home washing machines. They reasoned that the large-size boxes of laundry detergents could be reduced to the size of an aspirin bottle while still retaining the necessary cleaning power. A concentrate would have the advantage of reducing the manufacturing plant, warehousing, shipping costs, supermarket retail space and storage space in the laundry room. So an idea for a soap pill was conceived and one entry was a product known as Salvo (Procter & Gamble).

During the marketing research, each of the ten soap manufacturers conducted independent studies to determine the characteristics that the soap pill should possess. An element of the research was the suds capacity of the new concentrate. In other words, should it be a high sudser or a low sudser?

On the one hand, the high sudser had the advantage of appearing to be really cleaning. It had the disadvantage of upsetting those concerned about polluting the rivers and lakes, or even their own septic systems. The other alternative, the low sudser, had very few pollution disadvantages, but if you looked into your washing machine, you might wonder if the pill was really cleaning. It was a fundamental question about the ideal product characteristics, and the research conducted independently by all ten manufacturers concluded that 80 percent of the housewives wanted a high-sudsing tablet for its visual cleaning assurances.

Nine of the ten manufacturers interpreted the data and produced the high-suds product. They began to fight over that 80 percent share of the market, each eventually settling for an average of about 9 percent market share. Meanwhile, the tenth company, a clever little marketing-oriented firm, produced a good nonpolluting low sudser and captured 20 percent of the market.

Everyone operates from the same basic marketing facts, but when establishing marketing strategies, it is a good idea to "think small" in small businesses. If you are clever enough to pick a good niche, you might not need persuasive skills. *Being a big fish in a small pond is another way of saying market niching.*

The Dogs Won't Eat the Dog Food: The Importance of Product

In sales folklore, there is no more popular story than the one called by its punch line, "The dogs won't eat the dog food." In fact, I tried to trace its origins and found it impossible to pinpoint when it started. It has passed from generation to generation, reappearing in many dialects in numerous sales situations. I first heard the story more than 25 years ago when I served at the feet of marketing guru Ted Levitt. It goes something like this.

At a large national meeting of the marketing department and sales force of a major dog food manufacturer, the marketing manager and promotion manager are delivering long-winded speeches about new strategies designed to increase their market share. Unfortunately, the results of every marketing brainstorm developed at previous sales meetings have been disastrous. Sales haven't gone up, so the marketing staff now asks the sales force to help them pinpoint possible reasons.

"Is it our promotion plan? Our labeling? Our marketing plan? Our prices? Is it the lack of advertising? Is it the margin to our distributors? We are spending more money per unit on the dog food in promotion and marketing than our competitors. Why haven't we been successful?"

Finally, in the back of the room, an old salesman who has been fast asleep, falls off his chair with a loud thud. Everyone in the room laughs. Hoping to embarrass the salesman, the promotion manager marches up to the microphone and says, "Mike, you are one of our oldest, most experienced salesmen. Can you answer that question?"

But Mike has seen this happen before. He had been through four previous promotion managers and six redesigns of the package. He is a survivor, so he says, "Yeah, I know the reason. The dogs won't eat the dog food."

The message is very simple. All the gimmicks and all the marketing and strategy and persuasive techniques in the world won't work unless you have a product that the customer needs.

Not Everybody Buys

Entrepreneurial persuasion requires 99 percent perspiration and 1 percent inspiration. It does not require any desperation! The entrepreneurial persuader seldom hears the word no. If you want to convince someone, my rule of thumb, explained in Chapter 7, is that you must be willing to make at least 15 sales calls on a prospect. Only after the fifteenth call can you put the phone down and say, "OK, they don't want to buy. On to the next person." Not everyone will eat your dog food.

Ten percent of the people will never buy, no matter how often you call them. But there are 250 million people in America, and if one of them doesn't buy, that leaves another 249,999,999 prospects. So the fact that some dogs won't eat the dog food should not affect a powerful persuader with a purpose.

Selling Leadership

All good sales managers eventually face a classic dilemma, and how they respond to the challenge often determines how well they do. It's well known that the best salesperson seldom makes the best sales manager, yet companies inevitably promote their best salesperson to the position of manager. This causes a double whammy. First, the best salesperson is off the road and in the office—sales go down. Second, the sales manager is less than ideal—sales go down.

The same dilemma shows up in the sports world. A good player usually does not make a good manager. On the other hand, many great managers never attained great stature as players—basketball's Red Auerbach, football's Vince Lombardi and baseball's Casey Stengel, to name a few. The great manager is seldom a great individual performer in a specific sport, whereas entrepreneurs excel as individual performers. It's rare to find them successful as managers, teachers or trainers. Their ability to perform well with a minimal effort stands in the way of being an effective teacher or coach. A teacher or manager needs patience and self-discipline to bring the younger player along. The skills needed to be a good sales manager are often just opposite to the skills needed to be a good salesperson. It's the Peter Principle at work.

Another classic sales management dilemma is: Should I spend time with the best or worst salesperson? There is no one answer. It depends on where you'll get the biggest return for the investment. All too often the squeaky wheel gets the oil, and the new sales manager usually errs by spending an inordinate amount of time propping up the losers. Experience argues that helping the superstars do more is a better use of time. Rainmakers work best among their peers and have trouble with subordinates who can't seem to create even a drizzle.

. . . .

"He who has never learned to obey cannot be a good commander."

ARISTOTLE, POLITICS, 4TH CENTURY B.C.

. . . .

Before You Lead, You Must Pace

Leading follows directly from pacing. As you establish rapport with someone, you create a link that can almost be felt. Leading comes just as naturally as pacing. You've probably experienced being with friends late at night when you're not tired at all, but you're in such deep rapport that when they yawn, you yawn, too. The best salespeople do the same thing. They enter another person's world, achieve rapport and then use that rapport to lead.

If you want a cat to sit in your lap, do you shout to the cat to come there? Or do you have to coax that cat to bring him to your lap? Cat owners know the answer to this one, and they all agree you can't demand a cat do anything. People behave the same way. Ineffective persuaders can lose their prospects by being too pushy.

Pacing questions are almost always fact based. They are most effective in the form of response questions. Good persuaders are always good pacers. Pacing words have many meanings. Language is built up over time to handle all the nuances of a culture. That's why pacing questions are often specific to the culture and the language.

Language reflects a society's needs. An Eskimo has several dozen words for snow because to be an effective Eskimo, you have to be able to make fine distinctions between different kinds of snow. There is snow you can fall through, snow you can build an igloo out of, snow you can run your dogs in, snow you can eat, snow that's ready to melt.

Here are a few pacing questions:

- "Is this a new location for your company?"
- "How long have you been with the company?
- "As I came in, I noticed a whole new department in accounting there. Is that a new department, or has it just been moved here from somewhere else?"
- "Is it supposed to rain today?"

Great Leaders Never Push, They Always Lead

If you have ever tried to move a piece of string across the table by pushing the string, you'll observe that it balls up. But if you grab it by the other end and pull it, you can get the string to slide across the table in a straight line. That's leading, not pushing. Remember that Big Jim Miller gives every new employee a piece of string to keep this principle in the forefront of their thinking (see Chapter 5).

Here is the story of two shepherds heading two separate flocks of sheep in the Middle East. One of the shepherds moved the sheep by staying in the middle of the flock while controlling the sheep with his staff. He kept control by hitting the sheep and nudging the stragglers toward the middle. When sheep wandered, he ran out and pulled them back into the flock. At the end of the day, this type of leader is sweaty and exhausted.

The other shepherd managed to stay about a half mile ahead of his sheep, and the flock learned the direction to travel by his familiar silhouette against the skyline. No sheep ever got lost or strayed too far because the leader always stayed in clear view of the flock. This leader is seldom tired or overworked at the end of the day.

Selling Is the World's Best Profession

When I was the head of the management department faculty of Worcester Polytechnic Institute in Massachusetts, I used to ask my undergraduate students what they wanted to do when they left school. No more than 2 or 3 percent of them ever said that they wanted to choose sales as a career. They always had some higher and loftier goals such as law, accounting or a profession. When I went back and checked the alumni records of all schools, WPI included, I found that at least one-quarter of all alumni are in sales. Why do young people have negative images of salespeople?

I remember when W. Clement Stone traveled with me as a CEO Club speaker in the late 1980s. The legendary founder of several insurance companies and originator of the concept of the positive mental attitude (PMA) was 85 years old during his CEO Club tour. He gave me his business card which read, "W. Clement Stone, Salesman." He was most proud of that title. Too often the art of selling is downgraded because the leadership of the head salesperson is weak. You can't have a great team with a weak leader. That's why sports teams always change the managers of losing clubs.

• •

"The final test of a leader is that he leaves behind him in other men the conviction and the will to carry on."

WALTER LIPPMANN, ROOSEVELT HAS GONE, *1945.*

• •

Leadership Feedback

The single most underused element of effective sales leadership is feedback—especially positive feedback. People perform better when they have a positive self-image. Yet all too often, people get little feedback, positive or negative. This sends a message: We don't care about you. And when people feel that you don't care about them, they're not going to give their best effort. Why should they?

Tommy Lasorda, the manager of the Los Angeles Dodgers for four National League pennants and two World Series championships, told *Fortune* magazine:

Happy people give better performances. I want my players to know that I appreciate what they do for me. See, I believe in hugging my players, in patting them on the back.

People say, "God, you mean to tell me you've got a guy making a million and a half dollars a year and you've got to motivate him!"

I say, "Absolutely. Everybody needs to be motivated, from the president of the United States on down to the guy who works in the clubhouse."

• •

"The lead dog in a sled dog pack exchanges an unobstructed view of what's in front of him for a willingness to set the course."

• •

Entrepreneurs of Today

It's the simple and the symmetrical that hold beauty. The entire universe is built on this principle: Simple ideas stand the test of time.

Even now, the physicists of the world are seeking a grand unified field theory to make their lives simple. The holy grail for these scientists is the fifth force of nature, which will combine the other four forces under one umbrella. Even Einstein sought it, but no one has found it to date. The four basic forces—gravity, electromagnetic force, weak force (atomic)* and strong force—(atomic), have been identified for a long time—but scientists posit that four separate and isolated forces are not simple. Hence, there must be one force or one relationship that explains them all. There is an inherent logic in that appeal. It's romantic and it makes sense. Hence, the quest continues.

The same holds for persuasion. Everything important should be simple. Otherwise, it doesn't have lasting appeal.

---

*The weak force holds the electrons in their orbit while the strong force holds together the protons and neutrons in the nucleus.

9 *Mancuso's Twelve Commandments*

"None will improve your lot if you yourself do not."

BERTOLT BRECHT, ROUNDHEADS AND PEAKHEADS, 1933

Successfully growing a small business is an almost impossible task, and few people succeed at it the first time. As with rising within an Indian tribe from the position of brave to head of the hunting party and eventually to rainmaker, it takes motivation and persistence bordering on obsession.

I have developed twelve commandments to guide CEOs on the path to wisdom—the wisdom of the rainmaker. I chose twelve rather than ten in remembrance of my favorite scene in a Mel Brooks movie, *The History of the World, Part I.* As Moses came down from Mount Sinai with three inscribed stone tablets, he bellowed out to the masses: "I have spoken directly to God, and he has given me these fifteen commandments." As he spoke, he slipped and one of the three tablets in his hand fell and shattered. Thank God!

Twelve Commandments for the CEO

1. *Pick good people.* The philosophy of President Franklin D. Roosevelt epitomized this commandment. He claimed that he wasn't the brightest or most capable president, and, to make up for his shortcomings, he surrounded himself with talented people who became known as the "brain trust." His philosophy was to

137

lect good people, then give them freedom to execute their areas of responsibility. This philosophy gained favor during the Roosevelt administration, and it continues to be a great motivator in the business world.

2. *You never fire someone soon enough.* CEOs tend to believe that if they err in supervising people, it always seems to be in trying to improve underperforming employees. When they finally do terminate someone, they always feel that they should have done it months ago.

3. *A company's weakest vice president often shares the CEO's area of expertise.* Pity the vice president for marketing who reports to a CEO who came up through the ranks in marketing. Whether by accident or design, it seems that vice presidents in a CEO's discipline are seldom as effective as those in other areas. It's the sandbox syndrome as the CEOs with certain skills just can't help meddling in their old favorite sandbox.

4. *Use your company's mission statement as a touchstone.* The mission statement of an organization is the most tangible measure of a CEO's effectiveness. One CEO made a major impact on the acceptance and use of what had been considered a so-so mission statement by significantly increasing its use and understanding throughout the organization. This occurred one day when he casually asked an employee if she could recite the mission statement. She did so perfectly, and the CEO rewarded that feat of memory with an instant $100 cash. In a week, the whole organization had committed the mission statement to memory.

5. *Avoid the neutron syndrome.* This occurs when the CEO walks into a room at a snail's pace, but the employees perceive that a neutron bomb has exploded. You know, the kind where the building and equipment are still standing, but all the people are gone. CEOs should count to three before they enter a room. CEOs often judge themselves by their intentions whereas others judge them by their actions.

6. *Avoid the mushroom theory of management.* This theory advises you to keep everyone in the dark and throw a lot of manure on them. That may be good for mush-

rooms, but it's no way to grow an organization. Communication is synonymous with good CEOing. The need to know what's happening is crucial not only for employees but for outsiders as well. It's not just doing things right that counts; it's doing the right things and then communicating that vision to a wide audience.

7. *Lead, don't push.* There are two kinds of leaders. As explained in Chapter 8, the first type is like the shepherd who is in the middle of the flock pushing the sheep. He uses a stick to keep them moving forward. The second type also uses a stick but for walking. He is out in front of the sheep, who grow accustomed to following his silhouette against the skyline. He moves the sheep by creating a steady vision that inspires confidence in his followers. *A good leader causes people to have confidence in him or her. A great leader inspires employees to have confidence in themselves.*

8. *Learn to work with boards and advisers.* Here is a topic on which entrepreneurs and professional managers seem to split. The entrepreneurial manager generally does not operate with an autonomous board of directors. The professional manager does. This difference is generally resolved in favor of the professional manager. It's interesting to note that entrepreneurs on their second or third venture establish their boards at the outset of the business, thus demonstrating the key discovery' in these exchanges: An entrepreneurial manager with experience comes closer and closer to becoming a professional manager.

9. *Plan before you implement.* A professional manager of a growing business seldom allocates sufficient time for the planning function; an entrepreneurial manager almost never does. Hence, it's a formula of:

$$Value \times Commitment = Effectiveness$$

And as a rule of thumb, it's harder to raise the commitment score than the value score. Planning is the rational determination of where we are, where we want to be and how we are going to get there.

10. *Try to lead a balanced life.* CEOs on their deathbed seldom regret not spending more time in the office.* More often they reflect that the rest of life seems to have been shortchanged in the quest to build the business. There is no more exhilarating task than to grow a business, but too often this intoxication overpowers life's other needs.

11. *Make sure that objectives are clear and attainable.* Both the entrepreneurial and the professional manager agree that every person in a well-run organization can say:

   - I know what I'm supposed to accomplish and by when.
   - My boss has agreed to my objectives and has allocated to me the resources I need to attain them.
   - If conditions change, I can shift my effort and still attain my objectives.

12. *Know what motivates people.* CEOs have used stock options, profit sharing, bonuses and a host of razzle-dazzle schemes to spread the fire into everyone's belly (see Chapter 5). All motivational programs are good if they work, but which is best depends on the company and its situation. There is surprising consensus that the most "bang for the buck" comes from negative motivation, yet few CEOs consider negative motivation as an integral part of an overall motivational program for their business.

   Robert Collings, the founder of Data Terminal Systems, described the purchase of a $20 rubber chicken as the best money he ever spent. Every 90 days, the chicken was moved to the lowest-performing salesperson's office. As a result, no salesperson was ever the lowest performer for two quarters in a row. Shame is a powerful motivator.

---

*Thank you Richard Rodnick, founder of the Geneva Corporation, Newport Beach, California.

If you want to be a successful entrepreneurial persuader, you'll have to know these twelve commandments as well as— or better than—you know the ten from Mount Sinai.

Mel Brooks notwithstanding, in formulating my commandments, I drew upon one of Walter Hailey's time-tested principles of persuasion and on my own extension of his idea. Hailey's concept is called the *naturally existing economic relationship* (NEER). Mine is called the *smallest possible inherent advantage* (SPIA). Both are designed to help persuaders maximize their impact with a minimum of effort—the essence of rainmaking. The concepts were mentioned in Chapter 1 as basic tenets of entrepreneurial persuasion. Now let's examine them more closely as a foundation for my twelve commandments.

Naturally Existing Economic Relationships (NEER)

Hailey developed his NEER marketing system to enable him to sell more insurance faster, but the concept has a much wider application. In fact, I have found that you can use NEER to help you accomplish just about anything.

To understand how NEER works, first consider your naturally existing relationships (NER). You have many. Everyone does. Your friends in your church or lodge are NERs. If you are a member of the PTA or Lions Club, you have naturally existing relationships. CEO Club members have NERs. Your family is a NER, and so is your neighborhood. Think of other NERs in which you are presently involved. The list is endless.

Now add to the equation the word "economic" and you have NEER. With an economic component to the relationship, expand your thinking and count your NEERs. To help in this project, let's consider some of Walter Hailey's naturally existing economic relationships at the time he was struggling along as a new insurance agent (see Figure 9.1).

Hailey sold flour to wholesalers and grocers before embarking on a career selling insurance. His NEERs were grocery store owners and managers of food cooperatives. They were naturally existing economic relationships because these people were known to him and the economic relationships were

Figure 9.1   Example of NEER Marketing System (Naturally Existing Economic Relationships)

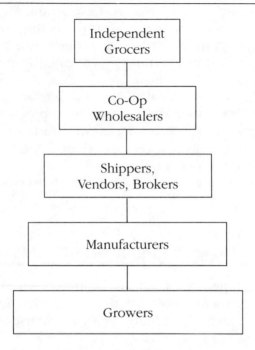

already established. He correctly assumed that if he could sell his idea to his NEERs, it would cause the leverage to kick in. In reverse, he reasoned, if you can't sell to your friends, who can you sell to?

Why not, he reasoned, market insurance plans to individual grocers through the same sources where they bought their food and supplies? His mission was to convince the wholesalers (the food cooperatives) to offer insurance coverage to the grocers along with other items. When a grocer buys meat, eggs and vegetables, why not buy insurance at the same time? When the client is billed for carrots, peas and lettuce, he or she can also be billed for insurance and can pay for all in one payment to the wholesaler. Do you see the economic relationship?

If you still think that it's illogical to sell your products through NEER, consider this.

A Canadian supermarket chain wants its customers to pick up their mortgages, mutual funds and checking accounts along with their muffins and milk at its stores. In a joint venture with Royal Trustco Ltd., the Loblaws Supermarkets Ltd., a subsidiary of Loblaw Companies, is creating a financial services company to enable shoppers at selected stores to do all their banking at their local supermarket. Though supermarket banking has been around since the early 1970s and has gained in popularity since the mid-1980s, the new company, called President's Trust, gives the concept a twist.

"From the beginning, we wanted to do something above and beyond the run-of-the-mill operations we'd seen springing up in the U.S.," says Jane Milner, a Royal Trustco official who is managing partner of President's Trust. President's Trust is the first time that a retailer and a bank have joined to create an entirely new institution to provide financial services in supermarkets.

Hailey later expanded this idea to wholesalers selling to beauty shops. Applying the leverage, he next used NEERs to sell insurance through other wholesalers. By repeating a success he had developed in the grocery industry, Hailey put into practice an old principle: When you have a success, repeat it over and over again. If you can sell insurance to grocers through their warehouses and wholesalers, why not sell insurance to beauticians through their suppliers?

To put it into his own words, he says, "When you have a success, pause to consider how many ways you can multiply that success over and over. Why go from a success into a new wilderness looking for new ways of doing what is already working for you?" It's a variation of the popular question, "Why reinvent the wheel?" Hailey doesn't believe in creating mediocrity when he can borrow genius. "Emulate, duplicate and replicate—or simply steal good ideas," says the master persuader.

Imaginative managers and salespeople in the auto club industry have successfully used NEERs to sell large volumes of club memberships through automobile dealerships. Disability income insurance is sold to attorneys through bar associations and to doctors, dentists and pharmacists through professional associations. We are encircled within other people's NEERs. We can put these principles to work for ourselves.

If you grasp this concept and carefully put it into use, you will have an opportunity to see just about any prospective client on a favorable basis. The methods outlined here make you an insider—that is, if you are a close friend of the person who has introduced you to the bank president, you will not likely be referred to a junior officer or be kept waiting in an outer office. Hailey explains that NEERs produce a "perceived equality," which is critical whenever two people meet for an important purpose. What could be more beneficial for the job seeker, fundraiser or any person seeking information or advice?

If you are a stockbroker selling stock by telephone, it's much easier to make that first call when you've been referred by someone for whom you have already been successful. The power of entrepreneurial persuasion drops off significantly when you have no existing economic relationship. It's all uphill. Oh sure, it can be done. But can it be sustained forever?

If you have no better or bigger opportunity than the next person, why are you doing what you are doing? Wouldn't it make sense to start working in an arena where you have some natural existing economic relationships? Entrepreneurial persuaders know that answer intuitively.

In essence, entrepreneurial persuaders always begin the prospecting with some form of referral. They start with a leg up. *Neither a wise man nor a brave man lies down on the tracks of history to wait for the train of the future to run over him.*

Smallest Possible Inherent Advantage (SPIA)

The refinement I've added to the NEER concept is also simple. Begin first with the situations in which you have the *smallest* possible inherent advantage, not the greatest. Complete all the small stages first before you move on the larger inherent advantages.

One of the best reasons to write a daily "to do" list is not to keep track of what you have to do. It's for the pleasure of checking off items that are completed. You feel so good when even the smallest item is done, don't you?

SPIA works well in a negotiation. You wouldn't begin a negotiation by tackling the toughest issue first because you might never get past that issue. It's better to accumulate a series of agreements on smaller issues to gather the momentum for the toughest ones.

Here's another example of applying the smallest possible inherent advantage. If you are successful with one company on the tenth floor of a building, why not then try other companies on the same floor? Then the ninth and eleventh. Then the eighth and twelfth. Do the whole building before attempting to work with the adjacent buildings—that's your smallest possible inherent advantage.

Tackle the easiest NEERs or IAs first—the ones that can be consummated quickly even if they don't offer the biggest reward. Let the big rewards wait until you accumulate the momentum gained with many small victories before you undertake the bigger inherent advantages. *That way you are combining a series of short winning steps to build a long-term success.*

I had an experience recently when I tried some NEER marketing with my CEO Club members. The principle was sound, but my methodology was not.

I wrote all the members asking for a new member referral in another city. I promised to treat every referral to a free lunch. I sent out 340 of those letters to my CEO Club members, but only about 30 or 40 of them responded by sending in the name of a good candidate in another city. That's not terrible, but it's hardly up to the level of NEER marketing. I felt that I should have received two or three times more referrals.

After refining Walter Hailey's NEER concept to the smallest possible inherent advantage, I tried a second letter. Instead of saying, "Do you have a friend in one of our other chapters?" I asked *specifically*, "Do you have a friend in San Francisco?" This question generated 100 replies. So over the next 18 months, I sent a series of specific letters to chapter members asking, for example, "Do you have a friend in Boston?" The results were staggering. These letters drew three times the response of the initial letter. About 90 out of 340 people sent back a lead saying, "Yes, why don't you invite so and so to a free lunch? He or she would be a good CEO Club candidate in Pittsburgh."

Even learning to swim is most commonly done in small, sequential steps. It is a misconception that you can teach a person to swim by dropping him or her into the middle of the lake. In practice, most people learn to swim by following a ten-step sequence:

1. Learn to blow bubbles in the water.
2. Learn to kick and blow bubbles in the water.
3. Learn to put your head under the water.
4. Learn to put your face under the water while kicking and blowing bubbles.
5. Learn to float on your back.
6. Learn to float on your stomach.
7. Learn to touch the bottom with your hand.
8. Learn to hold your breath under water for ten seconds.
9. Breath out and in with your face in the water.
10. Start to swim.

Of course, you might succeed by starting out with step 10, but doesn't it improve the odds of success to begin with the small initial step and then building confidence and momentum until you can swim?

As another example, if your service or product has been successful within a certain industry, why not call on the remainder of that industry before soliciting new industries? If your product has been successful in a certain geographic area, why not call directly within that geographic area and use the past successes from local companies as referrals? Again use the SPIA!

Why the Smallest Possible Inherent Advantage (SPIA) Works

Persuading people isn't easy, and most folks do it ineffectively. Rainmakers are good at it because they can assimilate and use SPIA. To make things happen, they begin with the arena where they have an SPIA, and then they move to the second SPIA, and the third, and so on. By breaking tasks down to their SPIA and getting each done in a sequential building block pattern, rainmakers are able to persuade more people than any other class of people.

And when an insurmountable obstacle appears, they use smoke screens to cover anything else that has to be done to gain the desired outcome. *They play the rules when they win; when they lose, they simply change the rules so they can win.*

The Importance of Hope

Rainmaker Barry Gibbs, a CEO Club member in Pittsburgh, describes himself as a hoper—someone who keeps hoping until he achieves his desired outcome. "Hope has proven a powerful predictor of outcome in every study we've done so far," said Dr. Charles R. Snyder, a psychologist at the University of Kansas who has devised a scale to assess a person's level of hope.

"Students with high hope set themselves higher goals and know how to work to attain them. When you compare students of equivalent intellectual aptitude and past academic achievements, what sets them apart is hope," says Snyder.

In devising a way to assess hope scientifically, Dr. Snyder goes beyond the simple notion that hope is merely the sense that everything will turn out all right. "That notion is not concrete enough, and it blurs the two key components of hope," according to Dr. Snyder. "Having hope means believing you have both the will and the way to accomplish your goals, whatever they may be."

You see, using your SPIA automatically increases your hope. Because you have a tool and others may not, you are at an advantage. Sometimes the SPIA is small, but it still results in more hope. That's powerful medicine.

Getting out of a Jam

The hope scale assesses people's sense of having the essential means by asking, for instance, whether they typically find that they can think of many ways to get out of a jam, or find ways to solve problems that discourage others. It measures will through such questions as whether people feel they have been fairly successful in life or usually pursue goals with great energy.

You need both the means and the will. All the skills to solve a problem won't help if you don't have the willpower to do it. Have you ever watched a good professional prize fight? Most of the top-ranked boxers are of relatively similar skill levels. The winner is usually the one who wants to win *more*.

Traits among the Hopeful

Dr. Snyder found that people with high levels of hope share several attributes:

- Hopeful people turn to friends for advice on how to achieve their goals.
- Hopeful people tell themselves that they can succeed at what they need to do.
- Even in a tight spot, hopeful people tell themselves that things will get better as time goes on. They don't consider quitting. It's not an option.
- Hopeful people are flexible enough to find different ways to achieve their goals.
- If hope for one goal fades, hopeful people aim for another. Those low in hope tend to become fixed on one goal, even when they find themselves blocked.
- Hopeful people can break a formidable task into specific achievement chunks. "People low in hope see only the large goal and not the small steps to it along the way," according to Dr. Snyder.

I trust that the preceding traits on hope help you make the correlation between hope and the SPIA. They both break formidable tasks into more manageable undertakings and then, like the beaver, they build the dam one twig at a time. They choose the dam site carefully, looking for inherent advantages. Rainmakers believe they can do anything, not just build dams or raise money. *They give out hope with their hype!*

Scales Measuring Lack of Hope

Many researchers use a scale that measures the lack of hope. The scale, developed by Dr. Aaron Beck and colleagues at the University of Pennsylvania, asks people how much they agree, for example, that there is no use trying to do anything in the future or that everything they try ends in failure.

Researchers who use the scale to study depression have found that, although hopelessness is often a subtle symptom, it plays a more central role in the psyche than other more prominent symptoms such as listlessness or sadness.

Research has even found that feelings of hopelessness are good predictors of how well people will fare in psychotherapy. Perhaps it is not a surprise that researchers have also found that hopelessness is the best predictor of who will commit suicide.

Figure 9.2 summarizes a few studies conducted by researchers showing the importance of hope as a predictor of success.

Telemarketing Using SPIA

SPIA works everywhere, all the time. It's a simple but powerful leverage concept employed by persuaders, and it's especially effective in combination with a telephone.

As in the examples discussed earlier in this chapter, telemarketing should be approached by tackling all the small items before you attempt the bigger ones. Before you launch even a small telemarketing sales effort, have your salespeople confer with telemarketers to design the sales pitch. This is an art, and professionals do it better. Then call potential customers in advance of mailing them a sales package. This improves chances of the package being read, and if they are not interested, you can drop them from the list and save on postage and follow-up calls. Finally, remember to call *after* a sale to ask for customer reaction to what you sold them. It is courteous, and it may net you additional orders. Following up cold mailings with a telephone call can also pay off and boost response rates.

Each step in and of itself is small, so you can capitalize on the small inherent advantages you have along the way.

Common Pitfalls for Telemarketers

On the Phone

"I'm sorry—she is on the other line." We've all ever heard that one. Here is a favorite answer. "Can you get a note to her

Figure 9.2   Summary of Studies of Hope

Researcher	Affiliation	Length of Study and # of Patients	Structure	Results
Dr. Lori Irving	Palo Alto Veterans Affairs Hospital		Hopeful video about cancer	Low hopefuls improved attitude and behavior.
Dr. Aaron Beck	Univ. of Penn.	Ten years 206	High hopers versus Low hopers	Level of hope was single best predictor of suicide.
Dr. Charles Snyder	Univ. of Kansas	3,920 college students	High hopers versus Low hopers	Hope level among freshman college students was better predictor of grades than S.A.T. scores or high school grade point average.
Timothy Elliott	Virginia Commonwealth University	57 people with spinal cord paralysis	High hopers versus Low hopers	No matter how long they had this disability, the high hopers had less depression, greater mobility, more social contact.
Robert Star	U. of Medicine and Dentistry in N.J.		High hopers versus Low hopers	They don't become hopeless if before contracting the severe disease they were high hopers.
Timothy Elliott	Virginia Commonwealth University		Nurses who care for paralysis patients	High hopers last longer on this job and do it better.
Dr. Charles Snyder	University of Kansas	7,000	Men and women between 18 and 70 years old	40% possess both will and means. 20% possess means but not will. 20% possess will but not means. 20% possess neither will nor means.

while she is on the call to let her know I'm calling back?'' If nothing works to break in on a telephone call, here are three guaranteed break-in suggestions. You may need to tone them down a little to actually put them to use, but they are guaranteed every time.

1. Does she want her swimming pool dug in the front yard or the back?
2. Where do I unload the truck with the gravel?
3. This is the attorney calling about the morals charge.

In a Meeting

When the prospect is "in a meeting," how do you respond? You should ask two questions: "How long has he or she been in the meeting?" and "How long do these meetings usually last?" Armed with this information, you may be able to try again more successfully.

Telephone Tag

If you can't get someone to respond to your call or to return your call, call back and say that you want to make an appointment. Again, ask the secretary two questions: "Do you have access to Bill's calendar?" and "Do you know when he'll be back?" If she says, "He'll be back at three," you can say, "Would you circle 3:15 P.M. on your appointment book, and I'll call back then to make an appointment, OK?" In this manner, you have used questions to break the big problem into a series of smaller problems so that you can gain the smallest possible inherent advantage.

Telemarketing To Make an Appointment: The Five Major Steps

1. Place all your calls from a referral. This is the first principle of telemarketing.

2. Tell the person that seven minutes is all you need for an appointment.
3. If the person says that seven minutes can't work, ask when you can call back because you need seven minutes.
4. When the person eventually invites you to spend the seven minutes in person, say: "I'll come at seven minutes to twelve and if you like what I have to say, you can buy my lunch."
5. If you can't get a minimum time commitment by phone, don't waste your time making the call. You can't sell everybody everything.

The Most Important Phrases in Telemarketing

1. Have you got a pencil?
2. Please read that back.

The reason these are the two most important phrases in telemarketing is that they involve the respondent in the activity. Involvement is the secret to success on the phone. Let's demonstrate.

Do You Have a Pencil?

The question is action oriented and implies that valuable inside information is about to be shared. It gives your prospect a chance to talk and a chance to say yes. When a prospect has both of these, you are on your way to success. The good news is that most people have some form of writing instrument at their desk.

Please Read That Back

You ask someone to read it back to etch it in his or her mind. At the age of 50, I am starting to be concerned about my inability to remember long telephone numbers with area codes and extensions. When I write it down and read it back, I triple my ability to recall it. *A short pencil is better than a long memory.*

Telemarketing Tips for Persuaders

Below are some effective telemarketing tips from Nancy J. Friedman's audio series, "How To Manage Your Telephone for Greater Profits." You can contact her at 800-882-9911.

1. *Avoid "emotional leakage."* Don't leak negative emotions from one situation to another. The person on this call wasn't involved with your last conversation, so don't take it out on him or her. If you're in a bad mood, take a deep breath and regain your professional composure before you pick up the phone.
2. *Answer the phone with your name.* People like to know who they're talking with. This holds true for internal as well as external calls. Use a healthy buffer (a friendly greeting) before you say your name. It indicates a warm reception. Zig Ziglar has his staff answer the phone with, "It's a great day at the Zig Ziglar Corporation." I've always wondered what they said on bad days.
3. *Never be too busy to be nice.* Being busy does not give you carte blanche to be rude or impolite. The caller doesn't know that you are on a tight deadline. However, if the caller says: "Hi, this is _____ . How are you today?" you can be sure that the caller is a telemarketer who is being impolite by imposing on your work time and concentration. To these, you should promptly say: "I'm sorry, but I never deal with bad telemarketers. Please cross out my name in your reverse directory." Then hang up quickly.
4. *If you are the caller to a business office, state your name and the purpose of your call upfront.* This may save time by connecting you with the exact person who handles that type of call, rather than having to repeat your request over and over through several departments.
5. *Answer your business phone with a smile.* This applies to everyone, from the CEO to the janitor. The smile can be seen and heard. The secret to good phoning is to be friendly before you know who is calling.
6. *Use your telephone receptionist as a buffer to the outside world.* When a caller asks to speak to the boss (by

name or title), the receptionist should always ask, "May I announce the purpose of your call?" No one likes to be grilled or challenged, but being announced sounds like a dignitary arriving at the President's Ball. Usually it will be something that the receptionist or another staff person can handle without bothering the boss.

7. *Be prepared for the called party not to be there.* Have a concise message ready. *The Wall Street Journal* reports that only 30 percent of all business calls get completed on the first try.

10   *Partners and Peers*

"Flocking together creates birds of a feather."

ALTON BARBOUR, PARTNERS & PEERS

"Mastermind" is the title of Chapter 10 of Napoleon Hill's classic book, *Think and Grow Rich*. It's the ninth step toward riches, and it's subtitled "The Driving Force." The whole chapter is only a few pages long.

It begins by stating that power is essential for success in accumulating money, and it concludes by saying that poverty and riches often change places. Poverty is bold and ruthless whereas riches need to be attracted because they are shy and timid.

Hill says that power is organized knowledge and that it can be obtained in three ways:

1. infinite intelligence
2. accumulated experience
3. experiment and research

The Mastermind

The "mastermind" is coordination of knowledge and effort, in a spirit of harmony, between two or more people, to fulfill a definite purpose. A mastermind has two components—economic and psychic.

The economic feature of the mastermind principle was first called to attention by Andrew Carnegie more than 50 years ago. Discovery of this principle was responsible for the choice of Napoleon Hill's life's work. Mr. Carnegie's mastermind group consisted of a staff of approximately fifty men with whom he surrounded himself, for the purpose of manufacturing and marketing steel. He attributed his entire fortune to the power he accumulated through this mastermind. President Franklin Roosevelt used a "brain trust" to enhance his knowledge (see Chapter 9).

The psychic phase of the mastermind principle is more difficult to comprehend. You may catch a significant suggestion from Hill's statement: "No two minds ever come together without, thereby, creating a third, invisible, tangible force which may be likened to a third mind." The human mind is a form of energy, a part of it being spiritual in nature. When two minds are coordinated in a spirit of harmony, the spiritual units of energy of each mind form an affinity, which constitutes the psychic phase of the mastermind.

Analyze the records of people who have amassed great fortunes, and you will find that they have either consciously or unconsciously employed the psychic and economic aspects of the mastermind principle.

For example, *Think and Grow Rich* (Hill) illustrates how one historical mastermind was formed. Henry Ford began his business career under the triple handicap of poverty, illiteracy and ignorance. Within the inconceivably short period of 10 years, he mastered these three handicaps, and within 25 years he made himself one of the richest men in America. Add to these facts the knowledge that Ford's most rapid strides became noticeable from the time he became a personal friend of Thomas A. Edison, and you will begin to understand what the influence of one mind upon another can accomplish. Go even a step further. Consider that Ford's most outstanding achievements began from the time that he formed the acquaintances of Harvey Firestone, John Burroughs and Luther Burbank (each a man of great brain capacity), and you will have further evidence that power may be produced through a friendly alliance of minds (see Figure 10.1). Again, this is a summary of the book *Think and Grow Rich*.

Help from Peers

At one of the CEO Club's morning roundtables, a member asked for advice on a current crisis. His customers and distributors had just received a mailing containing hateful and purposeful slander about him and his business. Written on fake IRS stationery, it mixed lies and facts; it was obviously ill-intended. His best guess was that a former employee (he had just reduced his staff by 30 people) or distributor was the perpetrator. The letter was especially damaging to him personally as it claimed that he had intermingled company and personal assets for personal gain.

Roundtable members were given a copy of the letter, which was thoughtfully sent to him by one of his best friends among his distributors. He put this question to the table of peers (all CEOs of different businesses): "What would you do if you were in my position?"

The discussion was heated, and solutions varied from legal to illegal actions. Everyone had an opinion, and a few had similar experiences. Then Don Buchholz, the CEO of a public company with more than 300 employees—Southwest Securities in Dallas—mentioned a related incident.

He recalled seeing a newspaper advertisement years ago by one of his favorite restaurants saying, in brief, "We don't use horsemeat in our food no matter what you have heard." Well, because there are about 10,000 other restaurants in Dallas, Don didn't choose this one quite as often. Up until that advertisement he had never heard a word about horsemeat.

After hearing this anecdote, members of the roundtable were unanimous in advising the CEO to ignore the slander. In hindsight, their advice was perfect. The CEO did nothing, and the issue was over in just a few days. Admittedly, this is difficult to do when you are emotionally involved.

Sounding out ideas, opportunities and problems with knowledgeable and involved peers is one of the best exercises you can do. It opens an information fountain that can make your ideas better. There is little downside to gathering advice in this way, for you are still free to choose what action to take. Rainmakers often consult chiefs and medicine men before they attempt to create rain.

Figure 10.1   Entrepreneurs of Yesteryear

Together in 1921 are entrepreneurs of yesteryear (left to right): Thomas Edison, John Burroughs, Henry Ford and Harvey Firestone. *From the collections of Henry Ford Museum & Greenfield Village.*

Problem Solving

Entrepreneurial persuaders are always open to outside opinions. They do not act emotionally or out of control. They gather facts, seek advice from trusted advisers, and only then do they make firm decisions. The sequence seems to go like this:

1. Define the problem.
2. Develop a list of alternatives.
3. Establish the criteria for solutions.
4. Seek advice from knowledgeable and involved peers.
5. Make a decision, and take action.
6. Take actions to reinforce the decision, and make it work.
7. Repeat the cycle again.

This process breaks big problems into small problems, which are always easier to handle. Step 5 is what seems to separate the entrepreneurial persuader from others who are also effective problem solvers.

Notice that step 4 above is the only one that theoretically could be skipped in the model sequence. It adds time, and the solution with step 4 included takes a little longer. But when peer discussion is part of the process, it lowers the probability that you'll have to tackle the same decision multiple times (step 7).

CEO Clubs as a Mastermind

In the ten CEO Club chapters across the country we have a form of mastermind to share ideas among CEOs. Each chapter meets eight times a year. These chapter meetings are a mastermind in and of themselves. The morning sessions offer private roundtables, which are opportunities to exchange ideas with peers. Lunch is almost always followed by a luncheon speaker or a group activity. This is actually a mastermind of a rotating group of people sharing ideas. It is a group of maybe 70 who appear on an as-needed basis to serve one another.

Within the CEO Club, we have a second, tighter mastermind concept we call a PAC (presidential advisory council). A PAC is a classic mastermind. Within a CEO Club chapter, about a dozen

CEOs agree to serve as a mutual board of directors and advisers for one another. Together they form an additional subset of the chapter. The PAC meets eight times a year, and each meeting is held at a different company location. The host company is always the focus of the meeting. The CEO Club provides a paid facilitator for this activity.

Lifetime Masterminds

· ·

"I have a lifetime contract. That means I can't be fired during the third quarter if we're ahead and moving the ball."

LOU HOLTZ, NOTRE DAME FOOTBALL TEAM COACH

· ·

When I set up the first chapter of the CEO Clubs in the early 1980s, I immediately offered a lifetime membership. My reasoning was simple. I planned to do this for the rest of my life, so why not open the same option to others?

This business, CEM and CEO, which I began in 1978, was sold to The American Management Association (AMA) in 1980. The AMA is one hundred times bigger and infinitely richer than I am. I bought it back in 1981, and I still vividly recall the discussion of lifetime memberships with the AMA accounting department, as the department explained clearly and logically that it couldn't and shouldn't be done.

So, as soon as I acquired the business back, I acted emotionally and offered the lifetime option. Not too many organizations offer lifetime membership, but I felt that it set a nice tone to the CEO Clubs, so I did it. The very good news is that more than 40 people whom I had never met before now form a unique mastermind for me.

They are in the system for a lifetime, too. I still don't know whose, mine or theirs, but I don't care. I use these people as an informal sounding board for ideas, and they have been invaluable to me.

The Persuader's First Mate

Since entrepreneurial persuaders are effective people with high achievement drives (I like to call them the "ready-fire-aim" types), which personality type works best with them? Let's examine a four-quadrant matrix composed of the following choices:

	Energetic	Lazy
Bright	3	4
Stupid	2	1

Look at number one, lazy and stupid. No need to spend a lot of time on this choice as anyone who is lazy and stupid shouldn't even be in private enterprise. They flourish in government.*

The second choice would be someone stupid and energetic, but this isn't a good match either. While we are empathetic to the stupid part, it's the energetic component that drives normal folks nuts. Incidentally, people who are energetic and stupid do not just work in government, they are government leaders.

Most people think that the third choice, someone who is bright and energetic, would be the ideal first mate for an entrepreneurial persuader. They couldn't be more incorrect. After all, entrepreneurial persuaders are also bright and energetic, and choosing a first mate who is just the same is like adding gasoline to a blazing fire. What the fire needs is a wet cloth to keep it in control and to act as a damper. Two bright energetics will spoil any activity. It's like having two captains of a ship, two orchestra leaders or two quarterbacks trying to run a sports team.

---

*The Lord's Prayer is composed of 50 words. The Gettysburg Address is composed of 266 words. The Ten Commandments have 297 words. And a recent government proclamation setting the price of cabbage had 26,911 words.

It can't be done. They have the same goals, but they always have different methods.

Of the three types discussed so far, bright energetics are actually the worst choice of all because they can cost you everything. In contrast, people who are stupid and lazy cost you only what you are paying them. Those who are stupid and energetic can cost you what you are paying them plus damages. Compared to someone who is bright and energetic, which could cost you the whole thing, they are both cheap alternatives.

Choice number four, people who are bright and lazy, are easily the most valuable commodity in the American enterprise system. We don't have enough of them. There happens to be an excess of entrepreneurial persuaders, but they are optimized only when they work in combination with a bright and lazy person. The shortage in the U.S. economy is not among the bright and energetics but rather the bright and lazies.

A bright and lazy person understands very quickly what has to be done. Full instructions are never necessary. However, the most valuable trait in this personality is really the lazy aspect. Lazy in this context doesn't mean no good; it means slow down.

How the Bright/Lazy Does It

Here's an example of the value of a bright and lazy vice president working for an entrepreneurial persuader who is growing a business.

As noted in Chapter 7 entrepreneurial persuaders like to arrive at work several hours early because that's the best time to sell. They have discovered that between six and nine A.M. they can get a lot of work done with no phones ringing and no one there to bother them. By nine o'clock, they have enough work compiled to keep ten people busy for a year.

A "bright and lazy" arrives at the office at around ten-thirty. The entrepreneurial persuader meets him or her at the door and follows the person all the way over to his or her desk, barking hundreds of instructions, commands, jobs and missions. He eagerly transfers piles of papers to this first mate and then heads back to his office to create another massive pile of work.

What does the bright and lazy vice president do with the first set of papers and instructions? Usually, he or she lets them sit.

By noon, the entrepreneurial persuader comes rushing back into the first mate's office with another massive pile of work. In excited tones, the persuader sweeps the first pile off the desk and places down the second. He says in a panting voice to the bright and lazy vice president (who is busy calling home, reading *The Wall Street Journal* or having a cup of coffee): "You know what I told you this morning? Forget all that."

In combination with a bright and lazy first mate, a rainmaker doesn't make any acid rain.

Masterminds as a Selling Tool

When you write a book, you have two fundamental choices. You can do such a good job writing the book that millions of people will tell other people about it, and it will become a bestseller. You won't need to rely on expensive marketing and promotion.

Tom Peters' first book, *In Search of Excellence*, and Peter Drucker's major book, *The Practice of Management*, are examples of business books that became classics with very little front-end promotion. Stephen Hawking, the physicist in a wheelchair, had a 40,000-copy first print run of his book, *A Brief History of Time*. It has sold more than a million copies. But blockbusters like these are rare.

The more common trend is the result of persuaders like Steven Schragis, the successful force behind Carol Publishing Group in New York. His firm's ratio of public relations people to editors is exactly opposite other publishers. He has more publicists than editors (eight to six), and that's unusual. Carol's shocking success with books like *Final Exit*, a guide to suicide, is a result of this reverse emphasis. The book is on its way to selling a million copies or more. During the first few months, however, the book had only sold 1,000 copies until Steven convinced a *Wall Street Journal* reporter of its value.

On the other hand, you could accomplish the same goal of selling a million copies of a book in another way, as one of the more successful business writers, Harvey Mackay did. His first book, *Swim with the Sharks*, and his second book, *Beware of the Naked Man Who Would Give You the Shirt off His Back*, are two examples of great marketing. MacKay wrote an adequate book, but then he did something brilliant: He sent the book to anyone who was anyone and asked to get a quote. Most book jackets have one or two quotes from standardized sources. He got quotes from unexpected sources like Robert Redford and Muhammad Ali, and then he used the first 20 pages of the book to summarize these quotes.

Consequently, before you read the book, you are preconditioned or preheated to believe that all these people like the book. If such a strong mass of people who normally don't promote books like it, it must be good. I call that a brilliant use of the mastermind principle to persuade.

Have you seen or heard Anthony Robbins' TV infomercial for his audiocassette program, *Personal Power*? He has sold over $50 million worth of that one product, making this one of the bestselling infomercials of all times.

How does he do it? The same way as Harvey MacKay, only better. Rather than just getting quotes, Robbins has legislators, movie stars and sports personalities give an unending stream of testimonials about the product. If you bought it and didn't like it—after all those superstars said they loved it—how would that make you feel?

Another example is Charles J. Givens, the author of the two bestsellers, *Wealth Without Risk* and *Financial Self-Defense*. *The Wall Street Journal* and a 1991 *Forbes* magazine article, "How To Market Mediocrity," say that his material is below average, but his marketing is unparalleled. Givens has sold 2 million copies of his books, and he claims to have a net worth of more than $100 million. He, too, uses the mastermind principle, and if it works for all these folks, it can work for you!

Masterminds as Mentors

Everybody needs a role model—one to follow as a guiding light. Women in the business world have been at a long-time disadvantage for lack of role models as compared to men. Mentoring has become an accepted way of compensating for this disadvantage, and I strongly believe in the mentor system. A mentor is simply a trusted adviser.

Finding a mentor is good advice for everyone wanting to go places. Walter Hailey proved the importance of mentors, and he recommends the idea to everyone attending his Power of Persuasion seminars. He likes to say, "Young people know they need mentors. The rest of us need them but don't know it as well."

One of Hailey's first mentors was a successful Dallas businessman who was many years older than the young, aspiring insurance agent. The man's name was Ben Tisinger. Hailey recognized that Mr. Ben was well known, had a favorable reputation in the business community and was well liked. Hailey reasoned that, if he could spend time with Mr. Ben, he would learn about business while being exposed to the man's valuable contacts, so Hailey offered to be his driver. Soon Hailey was seen in all the better places along with his mentor, who was careful to introduce young Hailey to all those around.

It wasn't long before others were asking Hailey if he could arrange an introduction to Mr. Tisinger. Hailey's mentor was a one-man *n*atural *e*xisting *e*conomic *r*elationship (NEER) for the new insurance salesman. Hailey made many valuable contacts while in the company of Ben Tisinger and benefited from his many sage ideas and suggestions. He literally showed Hailey how to make money.

One important caution about dealing with mentors: Never try to sell something to your mentors or to raise money from them. But don't be surprised if your mentors become interested in whatever you sell and buy it. Or if you are starting a new venture, you may find your mentors asking if they may invest in the enterprise. "Mentors are for advice, counsel and help," warns Hailey. "Never attempt to sell them. However, you should allow them to buy, if they ask."

Masterminds as mentors is a powerful concept and a key component in the arsenal of an entrepreneurial persuader. For more on this subject, I recommend a study of Andrew Carnegies's life and Napoleon Hill's book, *Think and Grow Rich*, especially Chapter 10, which focuses on masterminds. He says: "Whatever the mind can conceive and believe, it can achieve. Anything you can vividly imagine, earnestly believe in, and expectantly act toward—with God's help—must inevitably become accomplished! That which you're seeking is seeking you."

Others have said it like this: "When the student is ready, the teacher appears."

Mentors and Chauffeurs

The best mentor story I know is a derivative of Walter Hailey as a chauffeur.* It's about a physicist who spent his life studying quasars, black holes, neutron stars and Einstein's theories. This scholar gave numerous talks across the country and always stayed on the cutting edge of his technology. His lectures were awe-inspiring. Did you know that our sun has 99 percent of the matter in our solar system? If you add up all nine planets, including the earth, the sun is still 100 times bigger. Or, of the billions and billions of stars in the universe, many individual stars are over 100 billion times bigger than our sun. How does that make you feel?

His chauffeur (he called him a driver) had been with him for more than 30 years and was a companion and friend. The driver always sat in the rear of the auditorium during the speeches and on the way home gave his mentor advice on how the talk was received. His counsel to his mentor was a small reciprocal exchange for the lifelong friendship.

In his seventies, the physicist decided to deliver his last speech. On the way to the auditorium he said, "You know, it would be fun to have you deliver it for me. Do you think you could do it?" Because the driver knew the talk by memory he said, "Sure," and he was pleased to play along with the ruse.

He was excellent—even better than his mentor. He had good voice projection, and he thrilled the crowd. It was a huge success. Both the driver and mentor smiled politely during the extended applause at the speech's conclusion.

---

*I always wondered why the rich and powerful actor, Jason Robards, annually pays to renew his chauffeur's license. I guess he reasons that he has this skill to fall back on if all fails.

Then another physicist in the audience stood up and shouted out an unexpected question. "How do you see the similarity between what's happening in the universe and the field of particle physics? Do you see parallels with the planets orbiting the suns in galaxies and the world of quarks and quantum physics? Are you a believer in fusion or antimatter as a source of energy?"

The speechmaker was a little taken aback by this offbeat question, but his answer showed his resilience, which was one of the skills he learned during his lifetime with his mentor. "Gosh, that's such an easy question, I think I'll defer to my chauffeur, who is sitting in the back of the room. What do you say—will you answer that one for me?"

Masterminds as Influence Agents

The concept of smallest possible inherent advantage is closely related to the mastermind principle. When two or more minds are joined together in perfect harmony and directed toward a common purpose, a mastermind is created. A mastermind, in turn, can create relationships among the parties. It is amazing how many of these people now do business together as a result of being on one person's mastermind.

One of my mastermind friends likes to say that anyone using a mastermind principle is only seven people away from contacting anyone in the world.

Here is how he justifies the numbers. We have to round off a little because they're pretty large.

Let's say there are 6 billion people in the world in 1993 and that only 10 percent of them, about 600 million, are difficult to access. That means we want to reach 600 million people.

Now, if you have a mastermind of 100 people, and if each of these 100 has a mastermind of 100 people, and if each of those 100 has a mastermind of 100 people and so on, with seven levels of masterminds, we reach the startling number of 100 to the seventh power, or 100 million people. Hence, you are always only six or seven people away from reaching anyone in the world. (The math is correct; I double-checked it with a member of my own mastermind.)

What's more important than the number is the principle. A tight mastermind is a powerful outreach force for an entrepreneurial persuader. If you don't have one, you are operating with a bag over your head and one hand tied behind your back! *Your best helping hand is the one at the end of your arm.*

11 *Closing Techniques*

"He that speaks ill of the mare will buy her."

BENJAMIN FRANKLIN, POOR RICHARD'S ALMANAC

Zig Ziglar Closes

I have traveled the country with Ted Turner, T. Boone Pickens, Victor Kiam, Richard DeVos, Royal Little, Fred Smith, Edson DeCastro, Clement Stone and about 300 speakers who live and die on what they call "back of the room sales." Nobody did it better than the silver-tongued preacher from Yazoo City, Mississippi. Here is what I observed while the master was at work.

Principle 1: *Don't give the customer too many choices.*

Buying is an emotional decision. Customers often would rather have an expert say, "This is precisely what you need," than struggle through all the options. Zig packaged a clever combination of his various books and tapes in a neat shrink-pack with an easy-carry handle. You couldn't break up the package and price it economically. You either bought the package, or you didn't. There was little choice.

Principle 2: *Set the price at an optimum level and load the package with extras.*

Zig sold his package for $199. It didn't really matter that one book was $19.95 and another album was $94.45. The package

169

price was at the high end of the "afford" spectrum, and he loaded it with lots of extras. Of all the closing techniques he used, this was, in my opinion, the stroke of genius. It's what made everything else work.

Principle 3: *Allocate enough podium time to convince the customer of the value of your product.*

Most speakers use the last five minutes to hurry up and sell their book or tape. Some try to work it into the presentation several times and then tell you they'll make you a deal later. Not Zig. He used a full twenty minutes of a one-hour lecture to promote the $199 package. It was the centerpiece of his talk, not an afterthought.

Principle 4: *This is a one-time limited offer.*

He won't ship it to you within a week. He won't give you a coupon to mail in. He won't bill you and ship it later. You buy now, borrow the money from a friend if you have to, as this deal will be gone in about one hour. If you are going to move product, there has to be a compelling reason to buy right now. Later never works.

Principle 5: *Don't let the customers see how many products you have in stock.*

Hide the unopened boxes below the selling table. Create the impression that all that is left is currently on the table. Create the excitement that they may not get one. No one likes to be a fool who missed a good deal.

Principle 6: *Show your customers what they are getting.*

Picture four books and three large audiocassette albums. They are not alive. You can't plug them in or make them make noise. They're inanimate, but Zig gave them life in a full-fledged product demonstration. He had done this years ago for Salad-

Master when he demonstrated a gadget that sliced, diced and cut on TV. Using that same technique, he spent at least three minutes on every product. I came to believe that he could demonstrate a stock certificate as an exciting new invention.

Products don't have demonstrability. Salespeople do.

Principle 7: *Benefits sell products, not features.*

For each book or tape, Zig gave you at least five specific benefits. He overwhelmed you with benefits, and he anticipated objections. Here are a few of the benefits of owning his books and tapes.

- "Have you ever had a customer say the price is too high? Tell them 'I'd rather explain price once than quality every day for the rest of my life.'"
- "Have you ever had trouble closing a sale? This book is a little like killing a flea with a sledgehammer. I have a hundred closing techniques in this book alone, but when you're done with that flea, that sucker's dead!"
- "This tape is the one the astronauts took up with them to stay motivated while they were circling the Earth. Sure, motivational tapes wear off after a while, but so does a bath. Does that mean you shouldn't bathe?"
- (This is my personal favorite.) "It took me 16 years of selling pots and pans out of the trunk of my car to farmers in the backwoods of Texas, to get the ideas in this book. It'll save you years of driving around the hinterlands in search of a customer."

Principle 8: *After selling all the benefits of the individual products, sell the synergistic value of the whole.*

Zig says, "This is not a random collection of books and tapes; this is a lifetime library. A reference room in your house. I personally wrote and assembled this material specifically for people like you who don't have the time to wander around bookstores. You'll undoubtedly listen to this material many times. It's of timeless value, and because you already have it in the "ready" position, it'll be there when you need it most. And we both know there are times like that, aren't there?"

Principle 9: *Don't overlook multiple sales opportunities.*

Salespeople can lose a third of their sales by failing to remind the audience of friends and relatives who might need the product.

Someone told Zig that she bought a second set of his material for her son. Within a week the son had used it to get a new job. Her second purchase proved to be a better investment than an ivy league education.

Principle 10: *A professional is someone who gets better every day.*

Now that you have the tools to succeed, it's up to you to use them every day. It takes dedication to succeed at whatever you do.

The Puppy Dog Close

Isn't it strange that when the doorbell rings and the puppy goes to the door, it's never for him? Puppies never develop call reluctance. Each time the doorbell rings, the tail starts wagging, and off they go to answer the door. Even old dogs who can hardly walk never develop call reluctance.

Pet shop owners know this close instinctively. Why do they always put cute puppies in the windows? When you enter the store and show interest in a pet, did you ever notice how easy it is to get to take that pet home for a few days for free? They don't have to feed or clean them when *you* have them. It's a great close. There is no downside. Only opportunity.

Automobile dealers know, too, that anyone who takes the car home for a tryout is a great candidate to buy the car. Several new car dealers now heavily promote the test ride. Some say that the law requires a test ride (a half truth), or else the company could be exposed to product misrepresentation lawsuits. Obviously, the mere act of trying out a new car in a test drive significantly improves the likelihood of purchase.

Examine your own products and services. A free meal at a restaurant is a puppy dog close, isn't it?

Walter Hailey claims that he bought an organ at his ranch in Hunt, Texas, on a puppy dog close. The current owner said that he'd be glad to leave the organ behind when he moved if Hailey would like to try it for a few months.

It's actually easier to sell to a salesperson, isn't it?

• •

"Nothing will ever be attempted, if all possible objections must be first overcome."

SAMUEL JOHNSON, RASSELAS, *1759*

• •

The Classic Close: Encyclopedia Selling

When my wife Karla and I were first married, we received a telephone solicitation from an encyclopedia salesman. Historically, most encyclopedia sales have been made from cold calls or from door-to-door solicitation to homes.

Although the presentation was canned, our salesman used an absolutely brilliant close. It is a risk-reducing classic. It has to be to prosper over a long time with this door-to-door cold calling sales methodology.

The salesman said, "I've really enjoyed working with you as a couple, and I know you will get good use out of the encyclopedia. More than likely you are going to tell your friends, and because of you, many of them will want to have these books as well. I'll tell you what I'm willing to do. I'm willing to give you this whole $300 set of encyclopedias absolutely free if you will give me a letter of recommendation that I can use for your friends, if you will guarantee to keep the encyclopedia up to date and in good shape, and if you will tell as many people as possible about the value they provide for you. Now, if you'll agree to those simple things, we have a deal."

And you, as the customer, feel so excited for this special arrangement. Here you are, a chosen couple who are going to get a free encyclopedia that would normally cost $300.

When you look in detail at the contract, you discover what's really happening. The encyclopedia is free, but you have agreed to buy an updated annual volume every year for the next ten years at $45 an issue. This is a contract for roughly $500 over ten years or, in present value terms, about $300 this year—The same as the cost of the encyclopedia today. The salesperson reasons that if you are going to be a spokesperson for the encyclopedia, you naturally would want to have the updates so that you can remain current. Further, if you appreciate the generosity of the salesperson, you would certainly want to update your encyclopedia, wouldn't you?

So, again, what you see is a no-risk close. When risk is zero, money flows and transactions happen. The encyclopedia was never sold. It was just given away with the agreement that you would maintain it in the wonderful condition you received it in as a gift. That's only a sign of appreciation, not a cost of the product.

How To Work a Room

Do you ever feel stupid at a cocktail party or a social gathering? Have you ever noticed that certain people know just what to do? There's an old saying that some people watch it happen and some people wonder what happened. Rainmakers are the ones who make it happen.

What I am about to share was compiled from three sources:

1. Walter Hailey's *Power of Persuasion* seminar
2. CEO rainmakers at hundreds of annual lunches for our CEO club chapters
3. *How To Work a Room*, by Susan RoAne

Losers work a room by walking around the entire room, smiling and bobbing their heads up and down as they pass everyone. Winners work the room one at a time. They walk up to each person, firmly grasp that person's hand, look him or her in the eyes and say, "Hi. I'm Walter Hailey. Nice to meet you. I'm in the insurance business." The second hand clasps the hand he is shaking firmly. There is a touch, there is a style and there is eye contact. If you operate in that manner, one on one, it will take about an hour to work a room of about 60 people. When you have finished, unlike the loser, you will have identified all the prospects and found a few new friends.

• •

"The ultimate measure of a man is not where he stands in moments of comfort and convenience, but where he stands at times of challenge and controversy."

MARTIN LUTHER KING, STRENGTH TO LOVE, *1963*

• •

Flight Attendants

Have you noticed the commotion that occurs when a plane lands? While it's taxiing to the gate, passengers inevitably stand in the aisle to reach the overhead bins while the flight attendants work feverishly to get everyone back in their seats. It's easily the most frustrating part of their job.

Below are four phrases they can use to get the passengers seated. Rank them in order of their effectiveness.

1. *Plead.* "Please sit down. The plane is still moving."
2. *Light illuminated.* "Please remain seated and keep your seat belt buckled, the seat belt light is still illuminated."
3. *The FAA.* "The Federal Aviation Administration requires all passengers to remain seated until the airplane comes to a full stop and the captain turns off the seat belt sign."
4. *Accidents can happen.* "Please remain seated until the plane comes to a full stop because most accidents occur while the plane is on the runway."

I noted in Chapter 5 that the Roman orator, Cicero, always got a standing ovation after a speech, whereas Demosthenes got folks to take action. The same goes for this airline example. If you want a person to take action (like sit down), you'll be much more effective if you put away the microphone. Instead of yelling at all 347 passengers, speak directly, one on one, to the passenger who is standing. Then you can use all four arguments listed above, until he or she sits down. *Persuasion works best one on one, with touch and a direct personal appeal based upon reasons.*

Beggars and Fundraisers

The final example of how to work a room concerns asking for money.

Some subway beggars stand at one end of the car and shout out their pitch. (Some use a bullhorn.) Then they walk through the train with a cup. They would do better to ignore the folks who are not likely to donate and go one on one with the likely candidates (the old Pareto 80/20 rule, see Chapter 7).

Norman Groh, the CEO of Development Associates in Wellesley, Massachusetts, is one of the world's greatest fundraisers. He does it for non-profit and charitable causes, not to fuel entrepreneurial ideas. As a member of the Boston CEO Club, he recently shared his experience.

Always be specific; never ask for money in general. It's always best to ask for money by making it one on one: Your money will go to this kid, or it will buy the hospital x-ray machine, etc. Colleges never ask for money in general. They have specific scholarships (tall people, engineers, you name it). They will even let you put your name on a building, or a wing or a room. See how specific they get?

Groh says that it's hard to raise college money for the maintenance building but easy for all the rest. This CEO is so good at it that he has become the envy of the Boston CEO Club. Rather than using his wisdom to accumulate wealth, he stops work every month while the pile is still small. He then vacations until the end of the month. He averaged a week a month of work during the past ten years. He says that he can do this because he has learned to be a successful fundraiser by keeping his appeals very, very specific. He won't die rich, but he'll be smiling.

The Best Beggar in the World

Want to have some fun? During your next visit to Manhattan, treat yourself to a steak dinner at one of the world's premier steak houses, Palm, located on the east side of Midtown Manhattan (212-687-2953 or 599-9192).

On most nights, when you leave the restaurant you'll be approached by a good-looking man wearing a suit. He will say, "I was just robbed, and I don't have a penny on me. Can you give me money to call my friends for help?" It's a very powerful one-on-one appeal, and it has kept this person in the clover for a dozen years. He is a street person who has learned how to work a room.

What's sort of strange about this unfortunate man is that is all he has learned to say. This line works at such a high percentage that he has not had to learn to handle questions. He repeats his practiced and canned appeal to any questions and *increases* both the touch and the eye contact. This works best!

He has discovered (is he a "con"?) that this works better than answering follow-up questions because once you answer the first question, it leads to a second and third and *never to money*. He is wasting your time answering a lot of questions as a lot of people eat at Palm, and he is better off just starting over with a new couple. It's a faster route to money.

So now you know how to handle a room!

. . . .

"I think, therefore I am."

RENE DESCARTES

. . . .

Breaking into a Closed Circle of People

Let's say that six people are standing together having a private conversation. You want to meet one of them, but there is no obvious way to break into that circle. What do you do? I know a sure-fire way to break into a circle that involves both referral and touch. Don't blow it because if you do it wrong it can also backfire on you.

The first thing you must do is identify a referral for the person you want to meet. Then walk up behind that person and place one hand firmly (don't be afraid to be firm) on either shoulder. Even if the person is deep in conversation, because you have touched him or her, you are now on your way. When the person turns toward you, step firmly into the circle and immediately make eye contact. Then use your opening introduction to break in. "Don Smith, who is a mutual friend of ours, asked me to come by to introduce myself." Be sure to face the person you have physically touched in order to open the circle. It works every time.

How To Maximize Your Impact at a Sales Conference or Trade Show

Too many people complain "We don't get any business at trade shows, but we have to go for appearance's sake."

There are many ways to maximize your impact at a conference or trade show, but this one is a favorite because it's so effective and requires so little effort. At every conference there will be one night when there is no scheduled event. Usually that's the night the conference couldn't get any supplier to pay for a party. *That's your night!*

Arrange a small cocktail party at your place for that night and invite fellow rainmakers. Just rainmakers, as it should be intimate. This is a smart use of time and resources. For a nominal cost you can create an influence center for yourself. It allows you to use focused private invitations to gain power and prestige. If you do it right, you will soon be saying, "We do well at trade shows. We write a lot of business, and we like to attend them."

How To Close a Deal

I started this chapter with a detailed commentary on how the master salesman, Zig Ziglar, closes the sale. I'm about to close the "closing" chapter in the same way.

Investment banker A. David Silver has written a dozen books on entrepreneurship and addressed all CEO Club chapters with me a few years ago. His newest book, *How To Close Any Deal*, has this jacket quote from *USA Today:* "If entrepreneurship is a religion, then Silver is its high priest."

In his book, Silver identifies six steps to follow in closing any deal:

1. Find the DEP factor (demonstrable economic proposition) ignored by many sellers, to compel people to buy.
2. Determine what dealmakers should know to determine the best target for the sale.
3. Identify gatekeepers who can block your deal, and develop an effective strategy for "shunning their pikes."
4. Leverage others who can lose if the deal doesn't close.
5. Use appropriate questions to control the closing meeting.
6. Add a dose of third-party endorsement to the deal to provide the "myth of authority."

The book includes important guidelines for doing the necessary research prior to negotiations, including finding data on nonbuyers and closing one on one. It describes how to use directories, trade journals, library services and personnel—from the executive secretary to trade journal reporters—to target key individual buyers. Here is an excerpt from the introduction:

Many people are simply linear thinkers; that is, they assume that the only way from place to place is accomplished by taking one path, and that path must be the shortest, most direct route. Successful dealmakers learn how to think *associationally*; that is, they know that there are often several paths that will get them to their destination. When someone asks me to raise capital to shoot a movie, my first thought is not "Who's the director?" or "What's the size of the budget?" I want to know how many extras will be in the movie and what their ethnic persuasion is. Why? Because my Rolodex doesn't have the names and telephone numbers of many movie investors, but it does have the names of dozens of economic development directors from local communities with the capital to make loans or grants if a large number of minorities are hired as extras for six to eight weeks. By raising up to $600,000 in local development money, the producer can entice a bankable star and thereafter the millions of dollars necessary to shoot the movie. By thinking associationally rather than linearly, you can access the dealmakers that will say *yes* to the financing of your project.

You'll find out how to get to the heart of a deal: to put a "headline" on your premise to say: "this deal can solve this problem for these people." The *demonstrable economic proposition* (the DEP factor) is the single most important statement that persuades the buyer to write his or her check.*

This is also called rainmaker thinking, as it has a lot in common with the SPIA and NEER concepts. Isn't it interesting how two people can independently invent something at the same time (the steam engine, for example)!

How To Close Any Deal, by A. David Silver. ©1992. Reprinted by permission of the publisher. Prentice Hall/a division of Simon & Schuster, Englewood Cliffs, N.J.

12 *Entrepreneurial Winners*

"If you are in a battle you can't win, you should retire and start a battle you can win."

JOHN PAUL JONES

Winners accomplish more than other people largely because they are more persuasive. They convince others to share their vision—even when the vision is a mirage. How and why they do has been the focus of this book. I was going to make this the first chapter in the book, so it's all right if you elect to read it first as this book is organized like a circle.

To my knowledge, no one has focused on how these mavericks persuade. It's not just positive thinking that separates them from the pack. It's doing. Moreover, it's doing what convinces others to follow. They go with the flow, and where there is no flow, they create one. Then they go with that flow. *The old line that entrepreneurs play by the rules when they win and change the rules when they lose so they can still win captures the essence of persuasion.*

Persuasion is not manipulation. It's not simply selling, either. It's more a blend of selling, motivating and negotiating for a purpose.

How Winners Think

Two past CEO Club speakers were T. Boone Pickens, the legendary corporate raider, and Richard DeVos, the co-founder of The Amway Corporation in Aida, Michigan.

Both are big rainmakers in different worlds, and both spoke for no fee to our CEO Club chapters. Boone's best line was (call him Boone, not T. Boone, not Pickens, not T. Boone Pickens) "Not everyone likes me; in fact, quite a few people hate me. But I sure did make a lot of money for some people. You know, try as you might, it's hard to hate someone who made you a lot of money, isn't it?"

Richard DeVos has been listed annually in the *Forbes* list of the 400 richest people in America. In 1991, he was listed as number six, behind John Kluge (Metromedia), Bill Gates (Microsoft), the late Sam Walton (Wal-Mart), Warren Edward Buffett (stock market) and Henry Lee Hillman (Pittsburgh industrialist)—that's not bad company.

As DeVos was talking, someone interrupted and said, "You just plain have too much money. You are too rich, and it's not fair." DeVos glanced over at the person and said, "Oh, no, I'm not too rich. It's you. You are too poor. Why don't you get to work and produce something?" Then, in less than ten seconds, he returned to his main message. That offhand put-down wasn't preplanned. It was precisely how DeVos felt on the subject.

These examples show you how winners think. Their quick, unrehearsed responses to questions reveal what's really going on in their thought processes. These winners think positively, and they don't possess FAR. Remember, a winner is a person who wins, however that's defined.

Goal Setting and Achieving

Winners set realistic and achievable goals. Losers set either no goals or goals that are too high. Almost no one sets goals that are too low. Let's think of the goal-setting process in terms of a swimming pool. If a six-footer is going to learn to swim, is she better off being in a swimming pool with a water depth of two feet, five feet or eight feet? At eight feet deep, she could drown. Two feet of depth presents no challenge because her hands can touch the bottom. A depth of five feet is perfect because she can always stand up if she feels herself going under.

This reduces the fear of failure, which is what stops most people from learning to swim.

Achieving goals follows the same logic. Set them to be realistic and achievable, and you are on the way to being an entrepreneurial persuader. This ties in with the idea of purpose discussed in Chapter 1.

The Goal-Setting Process

If you ever have occasion to stop in my wife's home town, Elroy, Wisconsin, you'll see the whole town if you look both ways at the stop sign. A man once stopped at that sign and asked an Elroy resident, "Hey, do you mind telling me how you get to Milwaukee?" Her answer: "My nephew takes me there."

Not a very useful answer, was it? It reminds me of a story the late Malcolm Forbes* told about floating through a Texas cow field in his hot air balloon. He was terribly lost, but he managed to bring the balloon to about a hundred feet above ground, and he shouted to a local resident on the ground, "Help! I'm lost! Could you tell me where I am?" The resident shouted back, "You are about a hundred feet in the air in a balloon over a cow pasture."

Goals, like questions, must be specific. They must be measurable; otherwise they are useless. Dates and numbers make goals more measurable. Just saying that you want to increase sales is not as useful as saying that you want to increase sales by 10 percent in the next 12 months. Now *that's* a useful goal.

Goal-Setting Action Plans

Here are some activities winners use to set goals.

1. Seek group reinforcement from people with similar goals, and provide support to them in return.
2. List the benefits that you and others will reap through goal attainment. This will heighten your desire.
3. Review your goals daily.

---

* I love his tombstone, which reads, "When he lived, he lived."

4. Determine short-term goals by day, week and month. These incremental goals move you toward your long-term goals and enable you to measure your progress.
5. Celebrate triumph—reward yourself for each goal that is completed successfully.
6. Never give up! Strive, endure, persist, resolve with determination. *You have the stamina it takes to succeed.*

Priorities and Goal Setting

To be good is not enough when you dream of being great! One of the major differences between high-achieving people and people who only achieve well is their ability to set priorities.

The single biggest mistake people make in goal setting is to take care of the things that are urgent rather than the tasks that are important. I enjoyed the comment of one of our CEO Club members in San Francisco, who said, "Maybe it's a good thing that I am going slow, I just could be going in the wrong direction."

Goal setting is a vital part of winning! Without a goal, people perish. The person who fails to plan is planning to fail. The reason you set goals is to know when you have arrived.

Ten Characteristics of Effective Goals

1. Goals should be challenging but achievable.
2. Goals must be specific: not "to improve sales," but "to return to last year's level."
3. Goals should be quantitative rather than qualitative.
4. Individual goals should be linked to group goals. Groups goals should ultimately be linked to organizational goals.
5. Goals should be arrived at participatively. The people who must achieve them should have a hand in setting them.
6. Goals must relate to the success of the business, not to trivial issues.
7. Goals should be mutually reinforcing. One goal should not have to be achieved at the expense of another.

8. Goals should focus not only on ends but also on means. Attention to means is especially needed when setting objectives for employee performance.
9. Developing oneself and developing subordinates should be part of every manager's goals.
10. Goals must be written down. If it isn't in writing, it's not a goal.

Goal-Setting Exercise

I hope that by now you are convinced that goals are the first step to becoming a successful entrepreneurial persuader. Your goals need not be lofty ideals that require years to achieve. They can be immediate, focused and easily attainable. To illustrate, let's take time out to work through the following exercise.

Answer all the questions in writing, either in the book itself or on separate sheets of paper, with signature and date at the end. Make this a *living document*. That means reviewing your responses at least once a year (perhaps on New Year's Day as you are thinking about resolutions) and revising your goals as needed along the way to reflect changing priorities of life circumstances. Over time, you will have developed a useful record of your progress in becoming a rainmaker.

1. Rank your five most important goals for this year. (Why?)
   1. _____
   2. _____
   3. _____
   4. _____
   5. _____

2. Review these goals against the four rules of goal setting (answer yes or no):

   • Are they written in the positive?

   • Are they specific?

- Are they attainable?

- Can you measure them when they are accomplished?

3. Estimate when and if you expect to fulfill these dreams.
    Use dates and probabilities.
    1. _____
    2. _____
    3. _____

4. Inventory your assets (strengths). Don't worry about
    your liabilities (weaknesses).
    1. _____
    2. _____
    3. _____
    4. _____
    5. _____

5. Focus on times when you have successfully used these
    strengths. Make a list of at least three occasions.
    1. _____
    2. _____
    3. _____

6. Describe the type of person you want to become.

    _____
    _____
    _____

7. What prevents you from being that person today?

    _____
    _____
    _____

8. List three steps you will take to become that person.

    _____
    _____
    _____

9. Who are your mentors? Who are the members of your mastermind?

   _____

   _____

   _____

10. Create your ideal day.
    (morning)_____

    _____

    (afternoon)_____

    _____

    (evening)_____

    _____

11. Design the perfect environment for yourself—what would it be like?

    _____

    _____

    _____

12. Where do you want to be in 6 months, 1 year, 5 years, 10 years and 20 years from now?
    6 mos._____
    1 yr._____
    5 yrs._____
    10 yrs._____
    20 yrs._____

    _____

    _____

13. What things do you treasure most in your life? Rank in order of importance.
    1._____
    2._____
    3._____
    4._____
    5._____

14. If your doctor informed you today that you have only a few months to live, how would you make use of your time?

_____

_____

_____

15. Looking back, what activities have given your life the greatest meaning?

_____

_____

_____

16. If you won a million dollars, what would you do? What changes would you make in your life?

_____

_____

_____

17. If a genie granted you one wish, what would it be?

_____

_____

_____

18. What is your favorite activity?

_____

_____

_____

19. What have you repeatedly dreamed of doing in your life but have been reluctant to try?

_____

_____

_____

20. What has the highest priority in your life at this time?

_____

_____

_____

21. If you were guaranteed success, and *could not lose*,
what one thing would you do?

_____
_____
_____
_____

How Do We Get There? Practice

• •

*"The person who makes a success of living is the
one who sees his goal steadily and aims for it un-
swervingly. That is dedication."*

CECIL B. DE MILLE, SUNSHINE AND SHADOW, *1955*

• •

Setting goals is the first step in achieving. The second is practice. Winners know that practice doesn't make perfect. Only
perfect practice makes perfect.

Bill Parcells, the great coach of the New York Giants football
team, said, "For every minute a professional player plays in a
football game, he practices for one hour." That's a 60 to 1 ratio.

One quick way to get more done in the same amount of time
is to use all your senses all the time. You can hear while you are
doing other things. Most achievers, also known as winners, use
audiocassettes to complement their other activities. One of our
past CEO Club speakers was Mo Siegel, the founder of Celestial
Seasonings tea, in Boulder, Colorado. Mo built his business
from nothing and sold it for a pile of money. Then, a few years
later, he bought it back and has resumed leadership as the
herbal tea maverick. His competitors, who lost market shares to
Mo, used to call his company "the boys who are making tea
from the weeds by the swamp." They didn't like Mo because he
is a winner.

Mo is an avid audiotape listener. As we traveled on airplanes
together to the CEO Club chapters, Mo was never without his
Sony Walkman. He believes that he picked up an hour a day of

good tape listening in those long lines. I think this is a brilliant use of time.

So take a cue from Mo and use audiotapes to:

- Change drive time to thrive time.
- Exercise your mind while you exercise your body.
- Occupy your mind during bathroom times.
- Help you get moving in the morning or fall asleep at night.
- Record your vision and dreams. (It helps make them come true.)
- Dictate ideas while driving.

Winning While Failing

• •

"Babe Ruth struck out 1,330 times, but he hit 714 home runs."

• •

Mark Twain once said, "There is no sadder sight than a young pessimist." He's right. People who believe in failure are almost guaranteed a mediocre existence. Failure is something that is not perceived by people who achieve greatness. They don't dwell on it; they just keep moving forward.

In *The Sun Also Rises*, Ernest Hemingway's novel, Mike Campbell was asked how he went bankrupt. "Two ways, gradually and then suddenly," he responded. A lot of folks have gone broke two ways several times. Along with Mike Campbell, I count Milton Hershey, Henry Ford and Walt Disney as folks who failed while winning. And they say Henry Ford did it twice! That is, he went broke twice; he won only once.

When we recall the greats of the automobile industry, the same names always come to mind: Henry Ford, Ransom Olds, David Buick, Walter Chrysler and Louis Chevrolet. For decades, each Olds on a highway or Ford in a driveway has been a monument to the companies' founders.

But what about the less well-known entrepreneurs who keep their family crests off their goods? Are these innovators less worthy of recognition? Hardly. In fact, one of the greatest legends in automobile history is a person who's rarely spoken of today. William Durant was a winner who failed.

The Story of William Durant

From the beginning of his long career, William "Billy" Durant believed that a good product would be a self-seller. The product came long in 1886, when the 25-year-old Durant happened to ride in a road cart with a new kind of spring that smoothed out travel on rough roads. He borrowed $2,000 to buy the patent and formed a partnership with J. Dallas Dort. By 1901, the Durant-Dort Carriage Company, 14 plants strong, was the nation's largest buggy maker.

A zealous promoter, Durant was always scouting out new products. In 1904, he was invited to look at a failing company run by David Buick, a plumbing supplier and tinkerer. Impressed by an experimental car Buick had developed, Durant purchased the company. He is said to have financed the firm in a single day by selling $500,000 of Buick stock.

By 1908, Durant decided to form an auto combine. Incorporating under the name General Motors (GM), he proceeded to buy, with Buick stock, the Oldsmobile, Cadillac and Oakland motor companies. With nearly 30 companies under the GM umbrella, the business was valued at $37 million in 1910.

GM seemed prosperous, but the economy was fickle, the industry was young and Durant was too busy building to think about planning and safeguards. During the panic of 1910, GM found itself pressed for cash and a coalition of eastern bankers squeezed Durant out. This scenario is not uncommon in the lore of entrepreneurship, but what happened afterward is.

When Durant left GM, he took several long-time associates with him. In two years, they founded a half-dozen car companies, most notably the Chevrolet Motor Company (with racecar driver Louis Chevrolet). Durant consolidated the firms under the Chevrolet banner. By 1915, Chevrolet was valued at $80 million. Through the years, Durant had continued to buy stock in GM; by 1915, he controlled enough stock to retake the company.

Under his renewed tutelage, GM continued to grow. Among his acquisitions were a small refrigeration firm (christened Frigidaire by Durant), the Delco Company (adding the brilliant engineer Charles Kettering to his GM team) and the Hyatt Roller Bearing Company (adding Alfred P. Sloan to his GM team). GM built a $20 million office building in Detroit that was dubbed the Durant Building.

The postwar economy declined in 1920. GM, which only a year before had $38 million in cash, was now $200,000 million in debt. Durant lost more than $90 million—his entire fortune—trying to bolster GM stock. Shortly after leaving GM in 1920, Durant sent out letters to raise money for a new company, Durant Motors, which would strive to manufacture "a real good car." He had commitments for $7 million within 48 hours. His first car, the Durant Four, was designed and built in 47 days.

By 1927, Durant planned to compete head to head with GM by consolidating more than 28 percent of the U.S. auto manufacturers under the name Consolidated Motors. But when the stock market crashed in 1929, Consolidated Motors became a forgotten dream: Durant Motors was on the ropes, and Durant himself was nearly broke. In 1936, one of America's greatest entrepreneurs filed for bankruptcy at the age of 75.

Durant's accomplishments should not be diminished because he didn't leave a "Durantmobile" or a university endowment for posterity. He should not be overlooked, even if his spectacular building in Detroit has been renamed the General Motors Building. Despite the fortunes won and lost, Durant lived and died as an entrepreneur.

Do You Know This Loser?

Failed in business at age 21.
Was defeated in a legislative race at age 22.
Failed again in business at age 22.
Failed again in business at age 24.
Overcame the death of his sweetheart at age 26.

Had a nervous breakdown at age 27.
Lost a congressional race at age 34.
Lost a congressional race at age 36.
Lost a senatorial race at age 45.
Failed in an effort to become vice president at age 47.
Lost a senatorial race at age 49.
Was elected president of the United States at age 52.
The man's name is Abraham Lincoln.

How To Spot a Growth Industry

Winners are cutting-edge thinkers. They are able to spot trends, so they are usually part of the early group in any success. They make success happen, not by watching alone, but also by participating.

Let me share a technique rainmakers use to spot growth industries. It's a process, not a single solution. And as a process, it offers insight into how entrepreneurial persuaders succeed by being involved at the early stages of growth industries.

Watch the Magazine Racks

Did you ever notice that there are too many magazines on the newsstand and that they change quicker than an airline schedule? That's because a host of magazine entrepreneurs are watching trends. As soon as a new niche appears, it becomes flooded with magazines. Then over time, the good ones survive, and Darwin's principle of natural selection prevails.

You may not be interested in being a publisher of new magazines or newsletters, but you may find it valuable to know that certain new magazines were launched in a specific field. These tend to be early warning indicators, and futurists like John Naisbitt and others pay close attention to them.

Dr. Samir Husni, an associate professor of journalism at the University of Mississippi, is to new magazines what Kochel is to Mozart. His annual *Guide to New Magazines* is a comprehensive listing of virtually every new magazine published in the previous year. The statistics-crammed guide has become an important measure of pop culture. It can be found in the offices of many magazine publishers, advertising agencies, printers and trade publishers.

For the first time since Dr. Husni started the guide six years ago, there are fewer new magazines listed that in the previous year—536 in 1990, compared with 599 in 1989. Sex is once again the most popular category with 62 new publications devoted to the subject. The second largest category is lifestyle and service magazines, with 44 new titles, including *Swimsuit Trim in Just 12 Minutes a Day* and *How To Keep Your Family and Neighborhood Drug Free*.

Husni's *Guide to New Magazines* is available for $50 from the Department of Journalism, University of Mississippi, University, MS 38677.

Another good way to keep track of new magazines is by subscribing to *Folio*, the magazine for magazine management (*Folio*, 6 River Place, Stamford, CT 06907-1426, 203-358-9900).

You are off to a good trend-setting start by watching the titles of new magazines. When a magazine appears, it acts as a catalyst to spread and unite a trend. As a shared informational medium it pulls together the diverse aspects of a trend, and puts the full power of a hurricane behind it. This gives you a four-year lead time in spotting a growth industry. You can double that to an eight-year lead time by watching what magazines entrepreneurs read. For example, before launching *Inc.* magazine, founder Bernie Goldhirsch launched a magazine called *Sail*. However, he is not a soothsayer, and after successes with both *Sail* and *Inc.*, he failed with a handful of technology-based magazines.

Watch the Newsletters, Too

When an industry has a few successful newsletters, it becomes a candidate for a magazine. Before there was a clearly defined robotics industry, or a genetics industry, or a women's movement, there were newsletters in those areas. The magazines follow the newsletters.

You can monitor the flow of new newsletters from these sources:

1. The Newsletter Clearinghouse
    44 W. Market St., Box 311
    Rhinebeck, NY 12572
    914/876-2081

2. Newsletter Association of America
    Newsletter Publishing
    1401 Wilson Blvd., Ste. 207
    Arlington, VA 22209
    703/527-2333

3. The Oxbridge Directory of Newsletters
    150 Fifth Ave., Ste. 302
    New York, NY 10011
    212/741-0231

4. The Newsletter Directory
    Gale Research Company
    835 Penobscot Building
    Detroit, MI 48226-4013
    313/961-2242

Remember, winners are not always better *processors* of information but rather *procurers* of information. They are not necessarily smarter but better at figuring out how to get an advantage. For the would-be rainmaker, the difference can result in a downpour rather than a light drizzle.

Humor as a Winning Persuasive Tool

• •

"Money won't make you happy, but it will help you enjoy your misery in some darn interesting places."

WALTER HAILEY

• •

Whenever I am addressing a large audience, I like to work in a few one-liners—"God made only a few perfect heads; the rest

He covered with hair." This remark helps to endear me with my audience. You see, I have lost an awful lot of hair, and it's as noticeable as my weight problem. My general physical appearance ingratiates me with strangers because old, bald, fat people are not as threatening as Robert Redford. Selective, self-deprecating humor is a powerful persuasive tool.

I often talk about raising money, and in these speeches, I usually work in this line: "Since the beginning of time, God has created billions of people. He has made all kinds—short, tall, fat, skinny, one arm, one leg, etc. Yet during that same amount of time, God has never once made an over-financed company. All businesses at some time or another have to raise capital."

Humor is a release and laughter is a medicine. In the social experiment called Life, this can be just what the doctor ordered to turn a negative into a positive.

In his *Anatomy of an Illness*, Norman Cousins described how he made a miraculous recovery from a long, debilitating illness by laughing his way to health. Laughter was one tool Cousins used in a conscious effort to mobilize his will to live and to prosper. A major part of his regimen was spending a good deal of his day immersed in films, television programs and books that made him laugh. He found that immediate, positive physical changes ensued. He slept better, his pain was lessened, his entire physical presence improved.

Eventually, he recovered completely even though one of his doctors initially said he had a one-in-five hundred chance of making a full recovery. Cousins concluded: "I have learned never to underestimate the capacity of the human mind and body to regenerate—even when prospects seem most wretched. The life force may be the least understood force on earth."

A Real Laugh

Building a small business is often a disappointing process, when what starts out as a perfect dream turns into an imperfect reality. Any literature that passes along entrepreneurial wisdom while making you chuckle is thus worth mentioning. With this view in mind, I recommend J. Phillips L. Johnston's book, *Success in a Small Business Is a Laughing Matter*. Johnston is a millionaire and Horatio Alger type. Besides being a lawyer and serving on several boards, he is chief executive officer of Currier Piano Company; R. L. James & Sons, Inc.; Johnston Properties; and Chantry Ltd. He tells the following story in his book.

A friend and I plan to invest in a large cat ranch near Karmoville, Mexico. We would start rather small, with about one million cats. Each cat averages about twelve kittens a year; skins can be sold for about twenty cents for the white ones and up to forty cents for the black. This will give twelve million cat skins per year to sell at an average of around thirty-two cents, making our revenue about $3 million a year. This averages out to $10,000 a day, excluding Sundays and holidays. A good Mexican cat man can skin about fifty cats a day at a daily wage of $3.15. It will take only 663 men to operate the ranch, so the net profit will be over $8,200 per day.

Now the cats will be fed on rats exclusively. Rats multiply four times as fast as cats. We will start a rat ranch right adjacent to our cat farm.

Here is where the first-year tax break really comes in. Since we will be utilizing the rats to feed the cats, we can expense the entire first batch of rats purchased just prior to the year's end. If we start with one million rats, at a nickel each, we will have a whopping $50,000 tax deduction for the year even though the "cat rat" food will be used to generate income in the next year.

The rats will be fed on the carcasses of the cats we skin! this will give each rat one quarter of a cat per day. You can see by this the business is a clean operation, self-supporting, and really automatic throughout. The cats will then eat the rats, and the rats will eat the cats, and we will get the skins and the tax benefits! Incidentally, our ecology consultants think it's great.

Eventually, we hope to cross the cats with snakes. Snakes skin themselves twice a year. This will save the labor cost of skinning and will also give us a yield of two skins for one cat.*

Now that's a sample of the medicine called humor, and it's priceless! For some yet-to-be explained reason, God created only one species of animal that creates business and can laugh. When you are creating an entrepreneurial venture, you get to believe that God purposefully allowed laughter for humans just to act as aspirins for the people who manage businesses and the business of life.

Silly Ideas

Take time out to read the following silly ideas. These quiet, reflective moments can recharge your batteries and help take the edge off the unending quest to accomplish.

1. Couldn't we ship all the nonproductive people off to an island and let the rest of us enjoy life?
2. Wouldn't it be cheaper to raise the level of education of our people by shooting everyone who is uneducated?
3. Couldn't we cut down on airplane hijackings by issuing every passenger a gun? They could return them when the plane lands.
4. ABC News announced that former Soviet leader Vladimir Lenin's body was up for sale for $15 million. They attributed the source to the usually reliable *Forbes* magazine. It was a hoax, and both *Forbes* and ABC had to issue a correction.

Truth is stranger than fiction. A fairy tale starts out with "Once upon a time"; an entrepreneur's tale starts out — "You're not going to believe this."

---

*Excerpted from *Success in a Small Business Is a Laughing Matter*, 2nd edition, by J. Phillips L. Johnston. Copyright 1982 by J. Phillips L. Johnston. Published by Meridional Publications. Reprinted with permission.

Afterword

Joe Mancuso is the entrepreneur's best friend. He has dedicated his life to helping entrepreneurs to become all they are capable of becoming. His Chief Executive Officers organization and Center for Entrepreneurial Management are a great network of masterminds who meet to share ideas on a regular basis. He has had the courage to build one of America's outstanding business associations. Joe has the extraordinary ability to identify the problems that these people have and to help them find solutions. His books and articles have had a big impact on executives and entrepreneurs for many years. He is a great mentor to these who are making the American Dream come true.

This book does a good job of accumulating information for the entrepreneur to use to get more leverage out of all the tools that are available to multiply personal effectiveness. Since I was just a little guy, I learned about leverage early. I know that if I was going to make it, I was going to have to get more physical and economic power and strength. I soon learned that gaining leverage was not a mammoth task. It was just making those small adjustments, the 10 percent improvements, that changed $1 + 1 = 2$ into $1 + 1 = 1,000,000$. That is what the philosophy of NEER marketing is all about—leverage.

For years, I have been traveling the country, building companies and training people in diverse industries. Each month, hundreds of top business professionals come to my ranch in Hunt, Texas, to sharpen their persuasion skills through our Power of Persuasion seminars. All who have received their entrepreneurial training at Joe's feet have been exceptional students. One of the keys to successful entrepreneurial developments is the rare ability to keep an open mind. The greatest obstacle to new learning is previous learning. The first step is to venture outside the box of self-imposed limiting beliefs.

That is one of the first keys to the magic of NEER marketing. Many people confuse NEER marketing with referral-based selling or high-level networking. Based on previous learning and limiting beliefs, the first common reaction is "I know that." Anytime I catch myself saying that, I have to stop and ask myself, "Was I doing it effectively yesterday?" Just because we may be doing something does not mean that we are doing it to its peak effectiveness. If you keep doing what you have been doing, what makes you think you are not going to keep getting what you have been getting? The only thing that is not going to change in our world is that things are going to continue changing. The entrepreneur's job is to create that change and take advantage of it. It all starts with an open, inquisitive, searching mind.

One of the best mind-expanding experiences I have on a regular basis is working with my own mastermind group. It has been primarily responsible for the best ideas that have made the biggest impact on my life and my career. NEER marketing was born in one of my mastermind groups. I would still be back on the farm picking cotton if I had not been willing to open myself up to the ideas, criticism and influence of others with whom I could meet with in total harmony and expand my mental limits. Once those mental limits were expanded, I immediately noticed that the limits of my external world also began to expand. The power of the entrepreneurial mind can never be cultivated enough. It is the most powerful beginning for new creations.

The second obstacle to an open mind is FAR (fear, anxiety and rejection). Approval addiction creates a mentality of conformity that will stifle the growth of any person or organization. True rainmakers are those who don't just survive economic drought but take advantage of it to create showers of opportunity for themselves and others. The ideas you've read about, if applied, have the ability to help you create the rain without getting all wet!

Walter Hailey
Hunt, Texas

Index